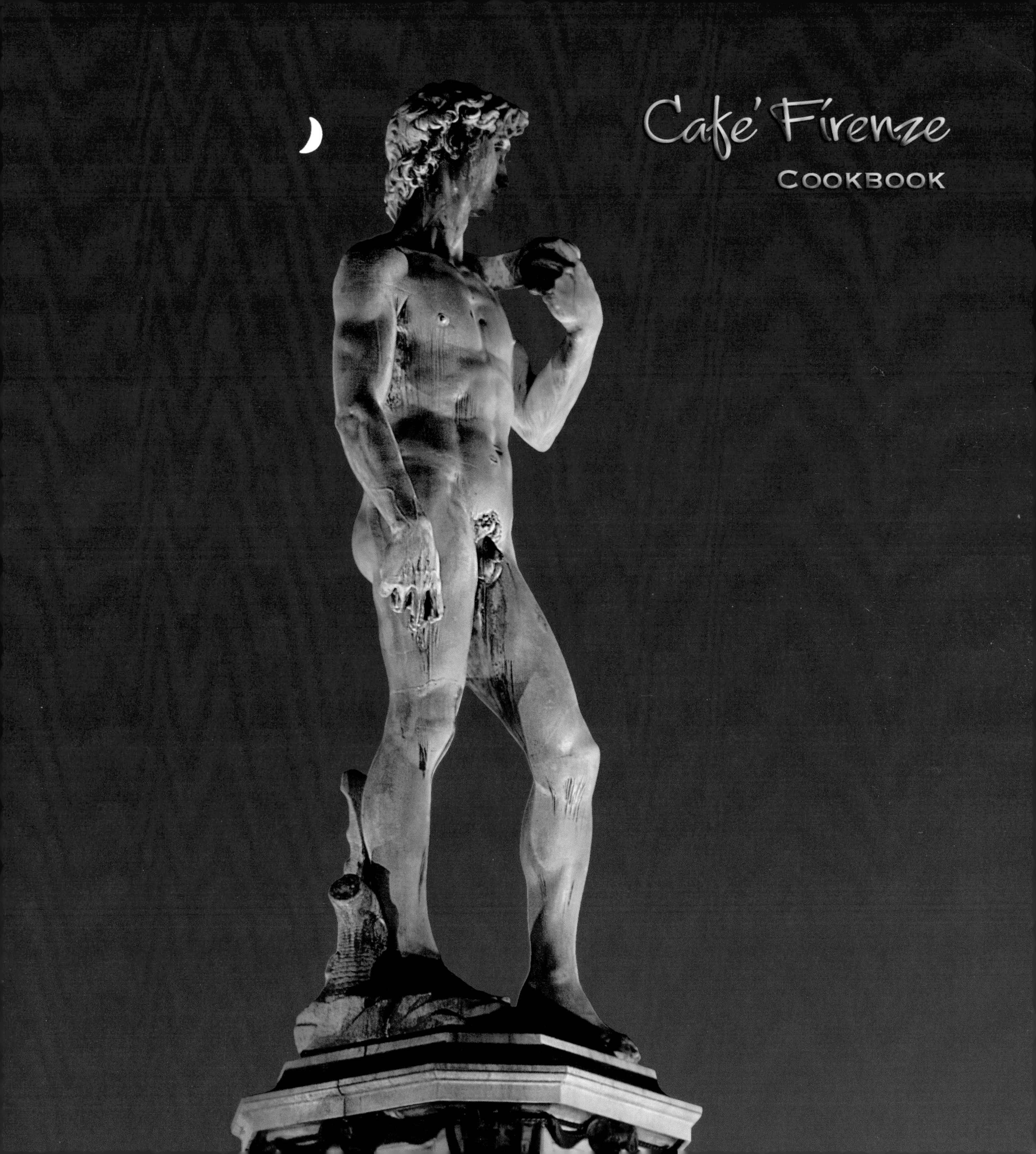
Café Firenze
COOKBOOK

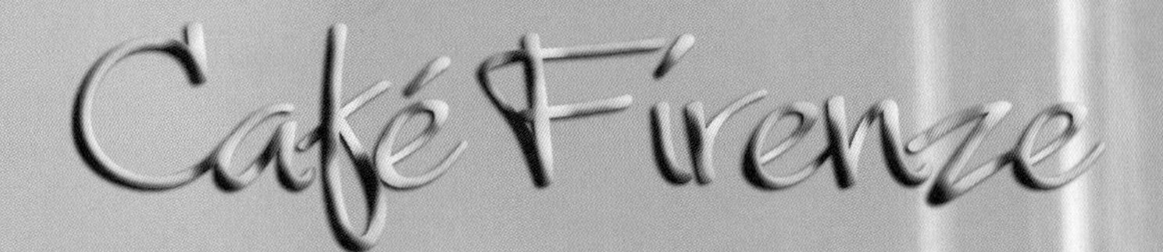

My whole life, for some kind of reason, has been centered around the symbol of the fleur-de-lis! Now, a lot of Americans know what that is, or have seen it somewhere, mostly because of the Da Vinci Code book, I think. But this attention is all good for my country, so... "Tutto Bene!" In the twelfth century, either King Louis VI or King Louis VII, history is still not really sure which one, became the first French monarch to use the fleur-de-lis on his shield. But I am proud to say that I have used it my entire life. It has always been with me, since I was born because it is also the symbol of Firenze! I even thought once of a comic book starring a character that could capture evil criminals by making drinks that would act like a truth serum and make people tell the truth. It's actually a real substance that has been around for years; it's called alcohol. I used to dream of being Superman, only instead of an "S," I would have the fleur-de-lis.

If you looked at my DNA, it would be a series of the fleur-de-lis! If I ever were to get a tattoo, you can guess the symbol. You get my point!

__Jacopo Falleni

Café Firenze Cookbook

Mangia & Bevi...

Food & Drink Recipes
From the Tuscan Sons

By Chef Fabio Viviani
&
Jacopo Falleni, Mixologist

Photography & Design By Antonio Busiello
Editing by Annette Ward

BRIO PRESS
Minneapolis, Minnesota

Library of Congress Control Number: 2009930381

First Edition

ISBN: 978-9819290-9-5

Printed in the United States of America by BRIO PRESS.

ACKNOWLEDGEMENTS

Fabio Viviani

I'm a Chef, not a writer; as a matter of fact now that I have to dedicate this book to somebody that inspires me, it's very hard for me, because, again I'm not a writer, so my inspiration came from the food and it seems stupid to dedicate a book to food and not a person.

I know that out there, there are some people that may be happy about this book. Maybe they are just going to think I'm an idiot. I can hear their voice in my head, "Look at Fabio! Does he think he is a writer? Get back in kitchen, Moron!" But, no matter what they think, those are probably the people that were working with me while I was writing this book, so this book is for them.

John Paolone, the most professional, hard working, and dedicated Executive Chef that I have ever had the pleasure of working with, thank you for running my (oops, our) actually yours more than mine, kitchen at Café Firenze so damn well. I would be nobody without you! I love you, man!

Abel and Kimberly, you are amazing people and it is incredible, and extremely pleasant to see how you both went from giving me headache to running my kitchen. You're the best!

Mike, Rosemary, Jessica and Austin, my only family in the United States. I thanked you already throughout the book, but I love you so much, so I decided to do it again!

My assistants, Bobbi and Kim, without you girls, I would be a sailing boat without wind! Where would I go? Thank you for putting up with all of my everyday requests!

Cherry, the best publicist on the market today, and to Britta her assistant, this book would not be possible without you. To Annette, for editing my book in such a gracious way and for making my retarded English intelligible for English speaking ears.

Antonio, man, I don't know anything about photography, but you took some damn great shots. I wish someday I could cook as well as you take photographs.

My manager Harry Gold, you are a rockstar my friend. I would be ground meat in a shark tank without you. William Shatner, not only are you one of the greatest actors in this country, but you have always been a true friend to me, this is for you and your beautiful wife, Liz and for our friends, Danny and Giorgio.

Dean Schaefer, my friend, I still don't understand how the lifeline technique works, but you fix my pain every day. You are one of my favorite people in the whole world. I am not gay, but I think I have a man crush on you, I love you, man!

Dr. Goldsmith and Father Gary, thank you guys, your words of comfort made me go through the end of this book much easier.

William from Retro SBK, man, you made some damn fast custom made motorbikes. It's a pleasure riding every Sunday on your piece of art. Craig, Anthony and Kiffen at Digital Imagination, my media life without you would be miserable. Andy, Dave, Valerie, Victoria and Suzanne and all the wonderful people at NBC /Bravo TV, thank you guys for taking such good care of me. Thank you to Jane, Dan, Nick, Liz and all the rest of the wonderful Magical Elves, you guys made me look really good on TV, thank you!

All my staff at Café Firenze, with you guys it's not business every day, it's a family reunion. And, for last but not least, to the person who wishes he was my brother, to Jacopo Falleni, thank you, man, I love you.

__Fabio

RINGRAZIAMENTI

Fabio Viviani

Io sono un cuoco, non uno scrittore, infatti adesso che devo scrivere le dediche di inizio libro, non so' da che parte cominciare, e quindi come faccio io a dedicare il libro a qualcuno se nessuno mi ha ispirato?
Ma ci sono delle persone alle quali sapere di questo libro fara' piacere, o magari penseranno che sono imbecille, ma comunque le mie dediche ho deciso che vanno a loro:

Alla mia mamma Renza, che non vedo l'ora di fare I soldi sul serio cosi ti mando in pensione e finalmente non ci dobbiamo preoccupare di operarti alle mani ogni 3 mesi e al mio babbo Valter, perche mi hai supportato e sopportato per tutti questi anni.

Al mio nonno Adriano per essere sempre stato ed essere ancora una delle mie persone preferite sulla faccia della terra, e anche se quando ero piccino ti dicevo che eri un rompicoglioni, oggi riconosco che senza di te non sarei la persona che sono, grazie, e porta per favore un grazie anche alla nonna Claudia, te che la senti spesso al cimitero, mi manca tanto e la rammento sempre, buttagli un bacio da parte mia, e non gli comprare I crisantemi che quelli sono fiori da morto, pigliali dei bei gigli, come quello di Firenze.

Alla mia nonna Gabriella che anche se hai piu' di 80 tu mangi sempre il fumo alle schiacciate e il sugo di carne buono come lo fai e non lo fa' nessuno, nemmeno io, e ti volevo solo dire che il Pollo arrosto che fai te qui negli Stati Uniti e' diventato famoso , e non so' come tu abbia fatto a non strozzare il nonno Renzo in tutti questi anni che non ha fatto altro che brontolare.

Al mio nonno Renzo che anche se sta' perdendo un po' di colpi ultimamente, credo che nessuno cela fara' mai a farlo stare un po' zitto, ancora mi fa male il collo se penso a tutte le volte che lo facevo diventare matto e lui melo stringeva fra le dita che non cela facevo neanche a muovermi, tieni duro nonno che a te non ti ammazza nessuno !

Allo zio Riccardo che te come me dalla vita qualche bastonata la hai presa ma alla fine siamo sempre in piedi e stiamo sempre lottando, e con te alla zia Cristiana, che anche per te la vita ne ha avute in serbo tante, e oggi telo dico, ti voglio bene e sei tra le persona piu' forti che abbia mai conosciuto, sei un modello di determinazione e testardaggine, e spacchi il culo a tanti e tutti giorni, sei la meglio, e guarda se tu mi vieni a trovare maremma puttana che tu mi manchi !

Allo zio Lucio che dopo aver scritto il libro, " come sfruttare un nipote ".... Mi ha buttato a largo nel mare e accidenti a te mi e' toccato imparare a nuotare, quella lezione poi mi servira' tante altre volte nella vita, e con te lo dedico alla zia Stefania, un'altra sorella della famiglia Talanti, un'altro carro armato, nulla ti piega e nulla ti spezza, stai lottando contro una brutta bestia, ma sono cosi sicuro della tua forza che come direbbe Ceccherini, " gli fa una sega l'acqua a l'uomo ragno !!!" Tieni duro, che te hai la forza per andare in culo anche a questa.

Ai miei cugini, a tutti e 3, Maddalena che finalmente hai trovato la giusta strada, ti auguro di essere felice con il tuo sposo, telo meriti, ad Emanuele, il mio grande cugino, ancora mi ricordo di quando avevi 5 anni e ti facevo guidare la moto..... te invece non ti sei sposato e se assomigli a me tu hai da tromabre un po' e via prima di sistemarti, e dammi retta, divertiti, e all'ultimo arrivato, Tommaso che da quando la zia e lo zio ti hanno portato via da quel canile in Romania che chiamavano Orfanotrofio dove ti tenevano rinchiuso, sei diventato il bambino piu' bello del mondo, anche se sei veramente agitato sei bello come il sole, un consiglio telo voglio dare, quando sei piu' grande magari lo capisci..... rallenta, datti una calmata, io ero peggio di te e ora mi fanno male I ginocchi e la schiena, calmati dai retta ad un bischero.

Anche se non lo leggera' mai questo libro, perche lui I libri non li legge lo dedico anche a Cristiano, il mio vero unico fratello, l'unico che abbia mai avuto, eri li con me l'unica volta che ho davvero pianto per amore, e grazie per non avere ammazzato quell ragazzo di Novoli che mi trombava la donna, a questa ora si sarebbe ancora in galera tutti e due...., eri li con me quando la mia nonna stava morendo, la stessa nonna che tutte le domeniche ci faceva il Pane e Nutella quando si era piccini, eri li con me quando venne la polizia, quando l'Italia ha perso ai rigori il mondiale io e te eravamo a San Vincenzo al mare, e eri li con me quando feci l'incidente in macchina ed eri li con me tutte le volte che fino alle 5 di mattina per colpa della troppa eccitazione non si andava a letto e si rimaneva a ballare, eri con me tutte le volte che succedeva una rissa, ma sopratutto eri l'unico con me a piangere alla stazione, quando sono partito per venire in America, non ho parole per dirti quanto bene ti voglio e quanto importante sei per me, sei una persona eccezionale, grazie di esistere e mi manchi da morire, abbraccia tutta la tua famiglia a dagli un bacio da parte mia, e ricorda che anche se siamo lontani io ti sono sempre vicino, nel bene e nel dolore.

Al grande " Nappa " Davide Montanari, che sei bello come il sole, e che se ero una donna , come dici sempre te, tela darei dalla mattina alla sera, e accidenta a te che se ti penso insieme a Cristiano non c'e verso di dormire.

Lo dedico anche al mio " Strucky " l'imprendibile Andrea " Cherino" Fiani che anche se l'assicurazione non funziona, te sei una garanzia e sei sempre avanti come il sole, una cosa tela devo dire pero', tagliati codesti baffi tu pari un terrorista..... e te mi devi dire icche' tu aspetti a fare le valigie e a trasferirti in America?

Ad Andrea Ballerini e alla Gatta e alla stupenda Alice, gatto mi manchi da morire, sarebbe bello avere un amico come te vicino, sopratutto ora, che consigli e buonsenso sono merce rara, grazie per I tuoi insegnamenti e la tua dedizione, sei un lottatore, non molli, e questo lo ho imparato bene da te, chi molla non arriva e quelli che arrivano non mollano mai, la vita ha grandi cose in serbo per te, valle a pigliare gatto, sono tutte li che ti aspettano, e ricordati che per te io ci sono sempre stato e ci saro' sempre, sei una delle poche persone che nella mia vita ha lasciato davvero il segno, uno buono, gli altri segni sono tutte cicatrici, mi manchi da morire e tutte le volte che ti sento mi emoziono, dagli un abbraccio al Pindo e digli di fare perbene, che senno' vengo io a mettervi in riga a tutti e due.

Alla Vale Amerini, la prima indimenticabile fidanzata che abbia mai avuto, io e te si e' aperto un'era che sara' impossibile da richiudere, ti voglio bene e spero che tu possa trovare qualcuno che ti sappia tenere a bada a che ti faccia stare bene allo stesso tempo, ricordati, per te Fabiolino c'e' sempre, ti voglio bene e non vedo l'ora di rivederti, e non ho mai avuto l'occasione di dirtelo ma mi sono sentito una merda quando decisi che non volevo piu' essere fidanzato con te quel pomeriggio a scuola e telo dissi per telefono, scusa.

All'Eli, Umina, Usmiani, non so' nemmeno come chiamarti, forse e' per questo che non ti chiamo piu', non saprei che cosa dirti, anche a te lo dedico, che a priscindere da come sia finita, sei stata una parte importante, se non la piu' importante, di tutta la mia vita, siamo cresciuti insieme ed insieme abbiamo fatto errori ed anche imparato, ad amare e anche a rispettare gli altri e forse e' proprio il rispetto che alla fine ci era venuto a mancare..... di te non ho mai avuto dubbi, sei una della poche persona che a Firenze e in Italia lasciera' il marchio, io c'ero per il tuo 110 e Lode, e ci credevo anche in quei momenti che nessuno ci credeva, adesso che non sei piu' un contaspiccioli, goditi la tua fama che tela sei meritata tutta, sei forte, lo sei sempre stata, e la mimma ancora non se ne rende conto di che mamma si ritrova, trattalo bene il tuo fidanzato e non sclerare troppo che non tutti sono capaci di reggere un talento come te, e quei pochi buoni, non sono piu' in Italia, stammi bene pezzetto e goditi la vita come io mi sto' godendo la mia, salutami Danielino e digli che per lui un letto cel'avro sempre se dovesse avere bisogno di scappare dall'Italia, salutami anche Enzo e la Leonora e strizza la nonna Fedora per me (ma non troppo forte). Siete stai una vera famiglia per me. Vi adoro.

A Matteino, che sei passato da essere un giovane arrogante e di talento ad essere uno chef con il tuo locale, bravo sono orgoglioso di te, se hai bisogno fischia, lo sai, per te ci sono sempre.

A Francesco Bonavolta, il mio unico e grande Chef, checco sei forte e sei sempre stato un amico anche quando ci sarebbe stato da incazzarsi, te eri li con me a pelare le Patate e Pulire la merda che gli altri ci lasciavano, ti rispetto tanto e ti ringrazio, in qualunque momento, chiama e io “stendo” il tappeto rosso.....

A Simone Mugnaini, per te sei il vero mito, in America e’ facile fare quello che ho fatto io, ma per farlo a Firenze ci vogliono I coglioni e te celi hai di piombo, ti auguro tutto il bene del mondo, e se oggi ho capito che cosa ci vuole per essere un ristoratore di successo e’ solo grazie ai tuoi insegnamenti e ai tuoi calci in culo.... Consistency, consistency, consistency..... ancora melo ricordo, e te poi sei come Giancarlo Antognoni, sei troppo pantera !!! Vienimi a trovare che non vedo l’ora di farti vedere che macello che ho combinato quaggiu’........ o Simo incredibile ma vero, la gente mi chiede di farsi le foto con me quando passo ! Macche’ si scherza davvero.......

Poi faccio un po’ di dediche generiche, a Luca Bracali che sei il solo direttore che abbia mai avuto, nonche il migliore fotografo sul pianeta terra, alla Francesca di Prato che mi facevi ridere quando tutti mi facevano girare I coglioni, ad Andrea Raugei che sei matto come un cavallo ma sei una forza della natura e arriverai lontano..... e una dedica la voglio fare anche al Cecco, il grande Cecco di Figline, la vita e’ buffa Cecco, ma la vita insegna sempre delle grandi lezioni, una di queste dice di non voltare mai le spalle ad un amico, disgraziato eri e sono convinto che disgraziato rimarrai, ma siccome non si gode mai delle disgrazie altrui, ti auguro tutto il bene del mondo.

L’ultima dedica mela lascio per una persona particolare, una persona che ho incontrato, incrociato e ritrovato in momenti particolari della mia e della sua vita, grande Valeria, si sto’ parlando di te, si sei te la Vale di Signa e lo so che in questo momento hai un sorriso che va da orecchio ad orecchio, che dire, sei forte, e sei bella come il sole, e te lo sai che io e te abbiamo tante cose in comune, cose che e’ difficile trovare a giro, Passione, Dedizione, Scopi, a tanto tanto cuore, facciamo parte della stessa causa, e a noi questa causa la ci piace da morire, quella delle persone che nella vita hanno una missione, avere successo e godersela, ed e’ una gran bella causa, siamo quelli che nel giro di 5 anni potranno decider se andare in pensione o no, se cominciare a godersi la vita, oppure continuare a dare alla causa....... Adesso smettila di ridere che ti ci vedo, tu stai ridendo da sola, ti pigliano per grulla, fammi uno squillo tutte le volte che passi da queste parti di mondo, che ti vedo sempre volentieri, e come mi garba quando ci si mette a ragionare io e te, non ce ne e’ per nessuno......un abbraccio.

L’amore e quello che provo per tutte le persone che hanno contribuito a questo successo e’ illimitato, purtroppo lo spazio in questo libro non lo e’ vi penso tutti e vi tengo sempre nel cuore, grazie ragazzi.

Le ultime due righe le scrivo per ringraziare tutti quei pezzi di merda che in un modo o nell’altro hanno cercato di fregarmi, truffarmi e approfittarsi di me, cercando di farmi passare per quello che non sono, scusate ma velo siete presi nel culo, chi e’ onesto vince sempre e le bugie vanno poco lontano.

Grazie a tutti voi, nemici vecchi e giovani, e’ sopratutto a causa vostra che decisi di lasciare Firenze, l’ho lasciata da sconfitto e adesso mi sto’ prendendo le mie rivincite e godendo di tutti quei successi che voi dalla vita non avrete mai.

Grazie di cuore.

ACKNOWLEDGEMENTS

Jacopo Falleni

Grazie! Yes, this is my way to tell you Grazie di tutto! Really, thanks to all of you! This book is the beginning of each of our personal stories. But the story, the story that we have shared with you, the story of Café Firenze was not the sole result of "Toothpick-Legs" Viviani and me. No, no, the truth is that this story is the result of many, many incredible people! The people I have worked with are the most amazing human beings I have known in my entire life. I have had the pleasure of working with the best of the best! Yes, you guys! I can't possibly mention you all by name (and that's a lot of blessing!). But I will try.

Starting from the two most important people in my life, Mamma Maria and Papa' Alfredo, who are still suffering from my decision to choose to succeed so far away from home! Thank you for making me who I am. You are my sample of life, my raw model; you are just perfection to me!

And, of course, I wouldn't be Italian if I didn't thank my very large, loud, loving, and beautiful family!

Grazie to my gorgeous "befana" Nonna Antonietta, who has been my hero since I was little. She was and still is the most cool Nonna ever. I remember when she picked me up at the kindergarten with her sport car. How I loved it. I was always saying to her, "Nonna, when I will be big and you will be old, I will buy a nice car like yours and I will drive you around, deal?" And she was laughing, laughing like crazy! Now I'm big, she is old, and the only thing missing is the nice car. This is the reason why I'm working hard so I can keep my promise to her! Incredible to think how hard and difficult life has been for her, but even more incredible is to see her still so positive! It is thanks to her that our family is so big and special: Seven aunts, seven uncles, fifteen cousins, and two bi-cousins. Good job, Nonna, good job!

And, thanks to Nonna Margherita and Nonno Elio that left us recently. I feel so lucky that people like them have made me appreciate the real value of life every day. Thank you for teaching me to love and discover the secret of the heart, the soil, how to plant, how to grow vegetables, about animals, the right moment for the harvest, and how to climb the trees to pick olives! Yes, behind those grapes and olives is a lot of work, love, and passion that makes Italy and Italians famous and proud in the World. Thanks!

A lot of time has passed and things didn't always go as we wanted in our life, but thanks for the opportunity that you offered to me. I was very young, yes, but my ideas were pretty clear, thanks to Antonella, Armando and Letizia!

I would also follow by saying thank you to my oldest friends, without whom I would not be the person I am today. Special thanks to Luca Picchi and Simone Mugnaini who always believed in me, the ones who taught me the love of my profession. Also, to Fabio Tongiorgi, Daniele Bacci, Fabrizio Giunti and il grande Nicola Langone, people I will never forget because they never forgot me. Being far apart didn't change anything between us. Thank you for letting me feel I could always count on you guys!

Obviously, I want to thank my friend, brother and business partner, Fabio Viviani, whom I'm sharing this beautiful dream with. Thanks for following me in this great trip. You will always be with me, on my shoulders! God you are getting heavy. My back is killing me!

I really need to thank a special group of people that can only be categorized as the family I never knew I had. Sometimes in life there are people who you come across who you think about later and say to yourself, "Wow! I sure am lucky I got to have that person in my life!" I don't know how I was blessed by being showered with wonderful, intelligent, loving people. People like: Mike, Rosemary, Austin, and Jessica. Thank you all. You and Fabio and I have truly formed a beautiful union!

Thanks to Christopher, Cherry, Annette and Antonello for helping me with this book. You guys are great and it has been a pleasure working with you. You made me think, learn and laugh, always telling me that if you tie an Italian's hands behind his back, he loses the ability to speak!

There are so many people I've been blessed to work with! My staff is incredible. People like Dan, Johanna, Ryan, Lisa, Tamara, Sandy, Mark, Jeremy, Mike, Jennifer, Antonio, John, Katy, Lizzy, Mele, Daniele, Damiano, Tricia, Stacy, Manuel, Alex, Jose, Roger, Ari, Luis, Jorge, Claire, April, Katie, Megan, Ryann, Kim and several more, too many to mention! But they all really are terrific people. A wonderful staff that makes every day a special one.

A special thanks to you, Brian. I knew you were a great person when you first started to work with me. You have such a great work ethic. But, believe me; I never ever thought you could be such an asset to my life and my business, as you have been. Thank you for every moment you have dedicated to me and to Café Firenze!

Life is funny. Things happen. Some say life is like a box of chocolate, you never know what you will get. But without one person, my being in this country would be very different. I will never forget what you did for me. I owe you for ever, thank you, Jennifer, and thank you little Noah!

The special Grazie goes to the person who taught me the most about loving people. He taught me to be passionate, to be a great host, and to learn that every moment is a special one. A person who is no longer on this planet, but will always abide in my heart. He is Francesco Del Pasqua. The boss that everyone dreams of and the one that I can say has truly taught me a lot in life.

Grazie a tutti! Grazie Francesco!

RINGRAZIAMENTI

__Jacopo Falleni

Grazie! Si cosi` si dice nel mio paese grazie di tutto! Ma ancora meglio grazie a tutti a tutti voi!
Questo libro e` l`inizio di ogniuna delle nostre storie personali. Ma la storia, la storia che dividiamo con voi, la storia di Cafe` Firenze non e` il risultato solamente della mia e quella di Fabio di storie.

No, no la verita` e` che questa storia e` il risultato di molte, moltissime meravigliose persone! Le persone con le quali ho lavorato sono le piu` eccezzionali che ho mai incontrato nella mia vita.
Ho avuto il piacere di lavorare con il meglio del meglio!

Si sto parlondo di voi, voi ragazzi! Non sara` possibile citarvi tutti per nome ma prometto ci provero`.

Iniziando dalle due persone, le piu importanti della mia vita, Mamma Maria e Papa' Alfredo...che stanno ancora soffrendo della mia decisione di aver scelto di cercare successo cosi` lontano da casa e da loro! Grazie di avermi fatto diventare quello che sono oggi, siete il mio esempio di vita, il mio modello, la perfezione!

E, certamente, non sarei italiano se non avessi da ringraziare la mia enorme, rumorosa, piena di amore e splendida famiglia!

Grazie alla mia bellissima befana La Nonna Antonietta che e` stata il mio eroe da quando ero piccolo, lei era ed e` la Nonna piu ganza , ricordo quando mi veniva a prendere all` asilo con la sua macchina sportiva...quanto mi piaceva...gli dicevo sempre..."Nonna quando io sono grande e te sei vecchia io compro una macchina bella come la tua e ti porto a giro ,ci stai?" E lei rideva rideva come una matta!(ora io sono grande lei e` vecchia l`unica cosa che manca e` la macchina...e` per questo che sto lavorando duro cosi posso risettare la promessa che le ho fatto!!!).
Incredibile pensare a quanto dura e piena di difficolta` e stata la sua vita ...ma ancora piu incredibile e` vedere la positivita che tuttora e` in lei!E`grazie a lei che la nosta famiglia e` cosi numerosa e speciale 7 zie, 7zii e 15 cugini...bel lavoro nonna bel lavoro!

E grazie alla Nonna Margherita e al Nonno Elio che purtroppo ci ha lasciato di recente,e grazie a loro che ogni mattina posso guardarmi allo specchio dove tengo le foto di famiglia e sentirmi fortunato che persone come loro mi hanno fatto apprezzare i valori veri della vita di ogni giorno. Grazie di avermi insegnato ad amare e conoscere i segreti della terra, come si pianta , come si coltiva come si allevano gli animali, quando e` il momento giusto per la vendemmia ,come arrampicarsi sugli alberi per la raccolta delle olive!

Si , quell`uva e quelle olive dietro le quali c`e ` tanto lavoro amore e passione che rendono l`italia e gli italiani famosi e fieri nel mondo Grazie!

E` passato molto tempo, forse le cose non sono andate come avremmo voluto, la vita e ` anche questo, grazie dell`opportunita che mi avete dato, ero piccolo ma le idee ereno abbastanza chiare grazie Antonella Armando e Letizia.

Seguo ringraziando, i vecchi amici , senza i quali non sarei la persona che sono oggi. Ringraziamento speciale va a Luca Picchi e Simone Mugnaini che hanno sempre creduto in me i quali mi hanno insegnato ad amare tutto del mio mestiere le cose belle e quelle meno belle. Ancora, a Fabio Tongiorgi, Daniele Bacci, Fabrizio Giunti e il grande Nicola Langone i quali non scordero` mai e che non mi hanno scordato mai, la lontananza non ha cambiato niente fra noi, grazie per sapere che potro` sempre contare su di voi!

Ovviamente, voglio ringraziare l`amico, fratello e socio Fabio Viviani, con il quale sto ` codividendo questo bellissimo sogno.... grazie di avermi seguito in questa viaggio......sarai sempre con me, sulle mie spalle, cazzo che mal di schiena!

Ho veramente bisogno di ringraziare un gruppo speciale di persone che possono solo essere categorizzate come la famiglia americana, la quale fino a 3 anni fa non sapevo di avere.
Qualche volta nella vita di ogniuno di noi ci sono persone che la attraversano ed e` soltando dopo che lo hanno fatto che pensi wow sono veramente stato fortunato di averle con me!
Grazie del vostro genuino e interminabile amore , Grazie Jessica, Mike, Rosemary and Austin

Grazie a Christopher, Annette, Cherry e Antonello per avermi aiutato con questo libro! Siete stati meravigliosi.... e` stato bellissimo lavorare con voi!Mi avete fatto ridere riflettere e imparare.... con voi ho capito che con le mani legate dietro la schiena non sarei capace di parlare ne` italiano e tanto meno inglese!

Wow ma quante sono le persone..... sono tante le persone con le quali sono stato fortunato di aver lavorato! Il mio staff e` incredibile.

Persone come Dan Johanna Lisa Tamara Sandy Mark, Jeremy, Mike, Jennifer, Antonio, Jhon, Katy, Lizzy, Mele, Daniele, Damiano, Tricia, Stacy, Tracy, Manuel, Alex, Jose, Roger, Ari, Luis, Jorge, Claire, April, Katie, Megan, Ryann, Kim, Katelyn e molte piu` troppe per mensionarle tutte!
Ma persone veramente incredibili. Un meraviglioso staff che fa di ogni mio giorno un giorno speciale e grazie a tutti voi di essere parte della mia vita!

Brian non ci sono parole per spiegare..... sapevo che eri una gran bella persona dal momento che abbiamo iniziato a lavorare insieme. Hai un incredibile etica lavorativa. Ma credimi non avrei mai pensato tu potessi fare un cosi grande cambiamento si, da spaccarmi i coglioni a gestire il mio ristorante!.
Grazie per ogni momento che mi hai dedicato e che hai dedicato a Cafe Firenze!

La vita e` buffa.... le cose accadono, qualcuno direbbe e` come una scatola di cioccolatini, non sai mai quello che ti tocca,ma c`e una persona senza la quale le esperienze in questo paese sarebbero state veramente differenti per me.non potro` mai scordare tutto quelllo che hai fatto per me ti devo per tutta la vita grazie Jennifer grazie piccolo Noah!

Il Grazie con la "G" Maiuscola va a una persona che mi ha insegnato ad amare gli altri ,ad avere passione per cio che fai ,ad essere un buon capo e imparare che ogni momento che vivi deve essere vissuto come se fosse l`ultimo! Una persona che non e` piu` su questa terra ma sara` sempre nel mio cuore. Lui e` Francesco Del Pasqua. Il capo che tutti vorrebbero avere e che posso dire di aver avuto Grazie a tutti! Grazie Francesco!

CONTENTS

Foreword

By William Shatner

Fabio and Jacopo are nuts. They really have a crazy streak. That, and they are Italian; it makes a very large splash in the small town of Moorpark, California. I met them because they started a new restaurant in the town near where my wife and I have our Quarter horses – by the way, the trainer is another strange Italian, Danny Gerardi, but that's another story.

We inched our way into this new restaurant in a mall, and mixed with the smell of fresh wood and fresh concrete was the smell of fresh...you name it, chicken, tomatoes, meat, cheese and don't forget the garlic– and then these two, good looking, young guys bound up and in thick accents cheerily asked us to sit.

Tentatively, I mean, eating is important to Elizabeth and Danny and me and we were having bad luck in the bedroom community of Moorpark, we chose to sit outside, it being a glorious California day and looked around. Florentine modern on the outside, Florentine Florentine on the inside. One of the two put a bowl of marinara in front of us, with some – guess what – fresh bread to dip in it and asked us how we were. We were famished. The three of us had just come from riding for three hours, practicing what we would have to do in the ring the next week and we were cowboy hungry.

"Why don't you give us something you like making?" I cautiously asked. Big mistake...and I mean big. Or should I say, plentiful mistake. Food on every corner of the table. Now, Liz and I have had our share of fine dining. Danny? Well, for God sakes, he's Italian, need I say more? We began to eat and each mouthful was an adventure, a journey. The meal was a trip; Moorpark would never be the same, and, of course, neither would we. The food was fabulous. The two fellows, who, over time became our friends, were like guides on our gastronomic adventure. Fabio and Jacopo, sounds like a vaudeville team, turns out to be no joke. They are stand-up proprietors of what is arguably (not by me) the best restaurant in Los Angeles.
Read on as to why.

--William Shatner

Antonio Busiello
Photographer

An Italian native and world traveler, Antonio Busiello was practically born with a camera in his hand. Whether above or below the water, he is easily found behind the eye of a camera lens honing his photographic skills and enhancing his collections.

His images have been featured everywhere from Animal Planet, to National Geographic and the BBC. After working on his doctorate in Anthropology and serving as an officer in the Italian Army, Antonio embarked on an unlikely adventure moving to the rural island of Roatan where he filmed thousands of hours of video of the gray reef sharks and the natural beauty of the Caribbean.

Today, with Los Angeles as his home base, he continues to travel the world. With camera in hand, do not be surprised to find Antonio shooting everything from nature to commercial photography, and from fine art to underwater.
See Antonio's work at: www.antoniophotography.com

I have traveled all over the world taking photographs. Where ever I am, I always look for good Italian food. As I live in Camarillo, California, I was pleased to find a restaurant run by Italians that served food the way Italians do in my home country. What a surprise to find them in my neighborhood. This is how I came to meet Fabio and Jacopo.

When they talked with me about photography for this gourmet food and beverage book, I was happy to join the team. It has been a great experience to work with them.

I want to thank them both for their friendship, their loyalty and of course for their incredible food and drinks. The flavor and the smells really take me back to Italy. And, there is no price for that!

Fabio Viviani

Owner - Executive Chef, Café Firenze
Born, Florence, Italy

Fabio Viviani is owner and Executive Chef at one of the most award-winning restaurants in the Ventura County area, Café Firenze, Italian Restaurant and Martini Bar, in Moorpark, California.

Born in Florence, Italy, he spent his first 25 years in his home nation traveling all over Italy and Europe in order to acquire the strong European culture of food, and trained in classic Italian and Mediterranean cuisine. He is also strong in creating dishes influenced by the European flair.

Fabio believes that cooking is a craft. Not being an artist that can paint and sell the work of one day for a long period of time, you have, as a chef, to work your butt off every day with consistency and passion.

He began his culinary career at the early age of twelve. Always asking for a chance to cook, he was given the opportunity two years later at fourteen when one busy night the chef cut himself badly; Fabio had the chance to prove himself. He has never looked back.

Fabio attended the Culinary Institute in Florence, Italy. Focusing on advanced Tuscan and regional cooking as well as a wide variety of specialization courses, he spent months, sometimes working for free, at regional restaurants and abroad to learn the secrets of master chefs.

Fabio co-owned and managed several high-volume Florentine restaurants and during the year received numerous awards. He also received highest recognition for his aged steaks and his cheese making abilities.

Fabio has organized food events for fashion shows by Roberto Cavalli, Alessandrini, Gucci, and others and acts as a consultant to several Florentine restaurants in the promotion of Tuscan fusion cuisine. Fabio has been personal chef for a number of Italian and international celebrities.

Outside the kitchen, Fabio enjoys soccer, fishing, and organic gardening. Every Sunday morning you will find him riding his Ducati motorbikes through Malibu Canyon with his wife and friends.

Jacopo Falleni

Owner - General Manager/Mixologist, Café Firenze
Born, Florence, Italy

Jacopo Falleni, General Manager/mixologist of Café Firenze, knows his business. He graduated with honors from the Instituto Professionale per I Servizi Alberghieri in Florence, Italy, where he received his technical degree in Hotel and Restaurant Management.

Since his graduation, he has honed his restaurant service and bar management skills by managing some of the most prestigious bar and nightclub venues in Florence, Italy, as well as acquiring a historic Firenze Bar and turning it into a local sensation.

Jacopo then graduated from Italy's AIBES, Association of Italian Bartenders, and was selected as an instructor for their bartending school. Competitive in nature, Jacopo has won several Italian national bartending contests and some of his garnishes have received top awards from the AIBES.

Addicted to challenge, his travel experiences have been some of his biggest. "I believe that travel is necessary to acquire culture and knowledge. That is why I jumped on the boat to the United States."

His first experience outside of his home country started in New York City. He opened the very first homemade Italian gelato store in Manhattan.

The store became very successful and started distributing to the finest New York restaurants and grocery stores, including Dean & Deluca.

Today he is one of the managing partners of Café Firenze, overseeing all restaurant staff and bar operations. He teaches his staff that business and life have a lot in common with a hug, "the best way to get a good one is to first give one."

Jacopo is currently working on a molecular mixology book, due out soon. Outside of the restaurant, Jacopo enjoys playing soccer, snowboarding, and surfing and has a huge passion for horses and horseback riding.

INTRODUCTION

By Fabio Viviani

Café Firenze is an Italian restaurant with approximately 250 seats and we have a huge bad-a** bar in the middle of the dining area, right when you walk in. We like to tell you, "let's go have a drink." Jacopo, my partner in crime, is an amazing bartender and mixologist. It is thanks to him that I'm almost an alcoholic (just kidding, and please, don't be stupid - don't drink too much). He came up with over 100 prime-quality-super-sexy martini ideas and he choose over 150 selections of the best wines in Italy and U.S.A. for the bar.

If you didn't realize it yet, I'm the other half of the problem here. I'm the Executive Chef, of course, which is pretty big yet simple, like a true Italian restaurant. All our plates are conceived from the best-of-the-best-of-the-best Italian tradition.

Our soup, salad, pasta recipes, the way we do meat and fish, are the result of over 500 years of hard work from other people in my country...I'm just carrying the honor of the tradition. Close to the restaurant we also have a separated area that we call our wine room. We do cooking classes and wine tastings there. It is also really good when we have a seriously big party, as it can be our private-room-on-demand.

We do everything on our premises. We do our own bread, we prepare our fresh pasta in the house, we age our meat in my 'nobody-is-allowed-to-touch-it' refrigerator, and my fish fly into my restaurant every day from one of the best fish providers in California. Most of the crustaceans and some fish are still alive when they get to my kitchen...how about that?

For our customers, each of our orders is prepared from scratch. And you know what, sometimes you may have to wait a little longer than you wait in the chain restaurant at the corner! I need time to give you the best food that you've ever had and you have to understand me. If you are in rush you may want to let us know and we will take care of that, but if you're not, just give yourself a break, stop complaining and enjoy the ride. If you have a son, you waited at least 9 months for him. So, if I take 30 minutes to give you the best steak of your life, I think it is worth it, isn't it?

Jacopo and I had a concept, but to be honest the curve of Café Firenze, the shape of Café Firenze, the Arch in the dining room, the corner here and there, the bar where you get all the great martinis, is my wife's work. She designed all of that. She is a really good architect, and believe me or not, she probably had to re-do the plan at least 20 times to make everybody happy. She is really patient and I love her for this.

She is really really patient with everybody...except at home of course. But you know what, I wouldn't be patient with me either. So what? I'm a Chef, I'm crazy and I'm way out there. I cannot always be present and logical and what I say most of the time doesn't make sense, thanks also to my just 3 years old English language knowledge. But I'm telling you if I'm in a good mood I'm the cutest person to be with, and she knows that. That's why she supports me!

She helped me a lot, especially at the beginning, when she was also hostess for me. I know how much she hates the restaurant business, she will never say that but I know she does so...thank you, anyway for helping us out and thank you also because I know how hard it is to work with me. I love you for that!

The décor, the color, the light, the material and the furniture came from the genius of the person that I define the best interior decorator alive, my mother-in-law. Armed with a company credit card and BMW Mini Cooper (red like a Ferrari) she turned all the shops in Ventura County, Santa Barbara and Los Angeles upside down looking for the piece, the door, the lamp, the masterpiece that will make you say WOW as soon as you step in.

So between me and my other two partners, Jacopo and Mike, we are...hold on...wait a minute...no, no, no...stop for one second...did I talk about Mike yet? NO? Shame on me. Honestly, how many of you know who Mike is? Does he exist? He is not somebody that we just pretend exists for taxes reasons. No, really, Mike exists, he lives, and he is here with us. What is Mike, an American man with Japanese origin, doing in Moorpark with two Italian expatriates half his age, with over 35 years experience in the restaurant business? Mike is the idea man. Mike is the mindset behind our action. Mike is the plumber in the middle of the night fixing (or breaking at worst) the sink that left us with no water in the middle of the Friday service. Mike is the painter. Mike is also the person that delivers our food. He is the person that keeps our finances and our sanity together, and last, but not least, he is also our biggest investor and the principal member of our company.

He is like a father for me. He is my example of peace and calm. He is a super quiet and relaxed person. He is so relaxed that sometimes when you ask him to do something several weeks can pass before he gets it done. The world can be falling apart around us and he will come up with a solution to cover our head. He is super politically correct. He will never do anything that can possibly hurt someone's feelings and he tries hard every day to make our life easier, happier and more profitable. Sometimes he can and sometimes he can't, but it's ok...He is our Mike, God bless him.

The only thing that I don't understand about Mike is the fact that he has a beautiful life, a nice wife, gorgeous kids, a great dog, a beautiful home and at almost 50 years old he decided to go in the most risky business with us. He started the idea; he believed in us from the first in this country. Mike believed in us, and if today, Café Firenze is what it is and is successful in this way, Mike is one of the main reasons. Without his incredible positive attitude and ability with numbers (did we get the P&L this month?) it would be way less easy, and we would be facing a way bigger risk.

I will work hard for him so I will finally be able to buy for him the Dream Boat that he has framed on his desktop. It is his dream and I will help him buy it...so he can get out of the restaurant and leave us alone.

Our expertise, passion for excellent simple food, and unique style of hospitality attracts local food lovers as well as those from miles around to our beloved state-of-the-art Café Firenze.

We also maintain a database on customer preferences so that when people return they can be assured they will get royal treatment, customized to their desires. For example, bones for dogs, special seating, etc. People will be valued and treated as special individuals.

Our place is definitely a destination restaurant.

__Fabio Viviani

INTRODUZIONE

by Jacopo Falleni

Wow! It seems that it's my turn. I'm sorry for sounding shocked; it's just that it's not exactly easy to get Fabio to stop talking! In fact, I'm afraid that if I pause for too long, he will start talking again soon!

Well, my name is JACOPO. It's not Jacobo, or Jacono, or Jacoco, or Yahoo, or Jacuzzi or any of the other weird names I keep hearing. Like a said thats Ja-co-po, or : Yah-coe-poe. Please-say it with me... I'm not kidding. Please! Say it with me...Yah,...Co,...Poe! Obviously, given my name, my mom nor my dad were not planning or ever expected me to visit the United States. Otherwise, they would have given me a name that would be slightly easier for Americans to pronounce! I'm getting so used to its mispronunciation; I sometimes screw up my name too!

I run the restaurant. I eat out to check new places out and get new ideas. I do research if I hear of any new martini recipes. I try to constantly keep myself updated on new products and services within the industry to keep us competitive, and, hopefully, stay a favorite of fine dining connoisseurs in our area. I hope that everybody out there can say the same about their own job! Salute!

I'm the General Manager and Beverage Connoisseur. "Chef in a Bottle," that's what they call me. I'm in charge of the front of the house, the bar, and the wine cellar of Café Firenze. I know that at this point, I may seem a little stressed. Actually, I'm not. In fact, it's just this level of hard work and dedication that brings out that special magic here at Café Firenze. Fabio and I love it so much that we even have plans to open up many more Café Firenze resturaunts in the near future. So we do work hard, but we've got a long way to go - and we're ready to rumble!

But I should make it clear that it wasn't always like this! Believe it or not, I don't come from Moorpark. I'm not a native Californian. And, if you've met me and heard my ridiculous accent: No, I was not born in the United States. No, the real story begins a lifetime ago. At the very least life's best memories just always seem to feel a lifetime away.

If I close my eyes I can still see vividly the color of the hallways of our Culinary School in Florence. I can still taste the food; I can still smell the classrooms. If you had asked me then, I would have told you that neither Fabio nor I would have ever known we would both end up working as partners in the same country, in the same town, nearly half a lifetime later. How could we have ever known the adventures in store for us, or the twists that life takes, placing us together (again), here in America!

Growing up as a kid in Firenze, I was lucky to already be in one of the best cities in the world! That is where we both come from, Fabio and I. And for you, Americans who have never been to Italia, Firenze is known to you as Florence. It's amazing and I insist that you visit it one day. Full of everything! Art, culture, interesting people, and oh yes: some of the best food and wine in the entire world! Anyway, as a kid I always dreamed of one day owning a restaurant and bar. I even used to get into fights with my friends when I wouldn't play along with our neighborhood games. My friends would argue: "Vogliamo giocare guardie e ladri. Chi avrebbe mai desiderato riprodurre cliente e barista?" (We all want to play Cops and Robbers!). Well, I can't blame them. After all, who ever heard of playing "Customer and Bartender?" But it's true. I always fantasized about owning my own bar. A place that I could name and decorate myself. I wanted to be able to scrutinize every last detail of the style and feel of my bar or restaurant! Since I was little I saw myself greeting my customers, seating them as they absorb the ambiance of my place, proudly describing to them the house special of the day, watching as they taste my drinks and ask how I did it. I never knew how truly lucky I would soon be.

In Italia, the culinary arts are considered sacred, and everything is based on the decision of where to go to school, which incidentally is where I met FABIO. And lemme tell you, he was this skinny kid, with legs that looked like toothpicks with a couple of feet at one end, and an innocent face that was any thing but innocent! Most American's know how seriously we Italians take our culture and cuisine. Plus it is fun for an Italian to do something with their hands. Something besides talking! But what most American's tend to not know is exactly how difficult it is to actually make these ambitions a reality. You see, in Italia, if one is to be either a chef, or bar/restaurant manager, one must have made their decision by age fourteen! This is because all of the best schools in our country for these professions are full institutional academies that begin at age fourteen. It is a one way street, a permanent commitment that takes almost six years to complete.

Furthermore, the student must choose before enrollment what their field of study will be. There are only two fields of advanced study. A student must either choose: Head Chef/Pastry Chef curriculum or the Bar/Restaurant Management curriculum. Five and a half years of study and one must decide before they enroll what to do with their life. So just imagine trying to figure out, by that age, who you are, what you stand for, and what you want to do with yourself for work. You can still choose other professions to study after that age, but if the culinary arts were your chosen path in life, you will have missed the bus. Luckily, I knew what I wanted to do with my life, and so it was in this place that I first met my lifelong friend, Fabio.

I can still see us now. Me, with my little whiskers unshaven and Fabio with his skinny white legs, trying to get into as much trouble as we could. From me pranking the bar by filling bottled with vinegar and putting baking soda in the shot glasses to Fabio setting alarm clocks to ruin our buddy's soufflés, we were probably the most troublesome students in the school's history. Believe me, it's a long journey through academics and into adulthood all being locked together in your studies for so many years! But a long way we have come from having being two kids running amuck down the halls of our beloved Scuola Aberghiera. Aside from our names, my sense of humor is the only thing that still feels like it did when we were kids. Well, that and Fabio's ridiculous little toothpick legs. We spent more time at the Boboli Garden than in English Lessons. We studied together, worked together, and consoled each other whenever one of us was suspended. And it wasn't long before we realized that somehow our future seemed destined to be spent together. We were so excited. The only question that arose was: "Could the world handle both of us at once?"

We had a blast in school and both graduated at nineteen, on schedule and with honors, I'm proud to say. We began our lives and I worked here and there, trying to make a living, trying to recoup the years of investment in our trade, always waiting for the doors of opportunity to open. Within a year, I had successfully complicated my life. I had my eye on a small but kinda famous bar with the same name as a famous Italian comedy: Cafe Amici Miei. I made the owner an offer (which much to my surprise, he accepted), and just like that, I finally had my own bar!

It was a small bar with only ten small tables that served lunch and dinner, but closed by 8 or 9 in the evening. I immediately had bigger and better plans, and started redesigning the bar to accommodate a more club-like feeling. I just knew that if the right people could see my work, they'd want to be part of it too, and hopefully would bring their friends. Let me tell you it wasn't easy. I went to sleep worrying almost every night about the food I was serving, the drinks I poured, what people really thought of me and my place, and most importantly, how to make it all better. Well, I must have looked like an Italian Martha Stewart to my employees because I was just as obsessed with the decor and ambiance of my bar and restaurant as I was the food and drink. But all my work somehow paid off because I started noticing the people responding to my ideas! They loved the fact that the bar was now open until early morning hours and had a club and disco type feel to it.

One night I was introduced to a businessman named Andrea who was a very well known importer/exporter of sports equipment. He had heard of my place from all his athletes and had come by to "check the place out." Within a month he had brought so many local stars and celebrities to the bar that I was a well known local person as well. He told me that he had a new concept for business in the US and wanted to be my partner. He wanted me to go to the United States to, (are you ready for this?) open a store in New York and sell Gelato! Keep in mind that at this point I am still barely out of my teens, so I had no idea what this meant, or how such relations can change one's life. When we met to discuss the deal, his offer included lots of money up front, all my moving expenses, a great salary, a chance to live in New York, and an opportunity to manage my own destiny, since the owner was now a close friend of mine. It was great, the opportunity I'd been waiting and simply "too good to refuse!"

Within six months I had accepted his deal and began my training to run Il Gelatone. Things were looking amazing for me, and I could not believe I was so lucky to have found such an opportunity. This is where I learned that life's education continues far beyond the classroom!

It's 2000 and I am the manager of one of the most successful first time gelato stores in the history of the city. On my opening day we had a line almost two blocks long! And for you Californians, I'm talking about two full New York City blocks. A long, long line. I couldn't believe it. The people of NY loved the store. They all enjoyed the authentic Italian feel. They felt like they were finally getting real Italian Gelato, and me with my thick Italian accent didn't hurt the image either. It was amazing! We had success, respect, good business and believe me the money was just pouring in! I mean pouring in! I couldn't believe that just selling Gelato would make such a vast sum of money. In fact, it was very hard to believe.

A very short while later New York was attacked. It was the last of my spirit. Even the city itself, the city I loved, was being destroyed. My faith in life and the good that could come of it was all but gone. Most of the employees quit, moved, or got fired. I moved too, and because of the effect the attacks had on all of us, my boss didn't question my motives. So with no job, I returned to Italia to work as a bartender at Bartender's Dream, my old mentor's bar. I had accepted my fate. It wasn't so bad, I told myself. At least I had my trade, my skills, and my health.

So back I am in Italia, this time it felt like for good. Working at my friend's bar was fun, and it paid the bills. But mostly it allowed me to relax and get my head back together. I was pretty angry at the world. My brain was still trying to reason the loss of all the momentum in my life, and I was trying to stay positive all day long. I just did my job, kept my head down, and enjoyed chatting with the patrons. In fact, I even met a nice businessman from America who came by the restaurant every day to chat about life, news, and my time in the US. Mostly though, he was interested about my time in the States. Little did I know that he was just pumping me for information because he was a restaurateur who was looking for a qualified person to manage one of his Italian restaurants in a place called Ventura, California. He'd been talking to me every day for two months, so he knew I had a valid passport and visa, and he knew I was ready to leave at a moments notice!

After Fabio and the rest of my friends picked themselves up off of the floor laughing themselves half to death, they asked the obvious questions: "You're going again? Why? What's wrong with you? Do you have brain damage? After what happened last time, why would you ever try this again? Why go back there? Didn't you learn your lesson?"

Well, I did come back! And I'm happy to say that it was for the best. I love the West Coast and immediately fell in love with Ventura. I accepted the job and served for just over three years as the General Manager of a small franchise and was even able to bring a friend in! Around the end of 2005, we needed a Head Chef and so obviously I called the most qualified person I knew, never dreaming for once that he'd ever even entertain my offer. But I was pleasantly surprised when he told me that he needed a change of pace. What better time could there be to reunite the Firenze boys back together, this time with a new frontier to face!

Since that day nearly two years have gone by, and now our lives are a little different. Actually, this is a lie because our lives never changed. We started working like dogs years ago and we still are working like dogs! After working and saving together, we went into business for ourselves. This time with the help of Grande Mike, Fabio's father-in-law, we started our own little (9000 square feet) experiment in Moorpark. We named the restaurant after our own first love. We named it after the place that birthed us, the place in both our hearts. CAFÉ FIRENZE opened in Moorpark, California in the summer of 2007 as a little delicatessen with three small tables. We were short of space; our little FIRENZE at the time had no advertising budget, no consistent clientele, and no familiarity with our new town of business. But, despite the imperfections, we had all that we needed.

We had our hope. We had our education, our craft, and our skills. We had our friends, both new and old, wishing the best for us. We had our dream. We had our love of hospitality, service, and entertaining our guests. And most significantly we had the one ingredient that ended up being the most important one of all! We had us!

__Jacopo Falleni

The Food

By Fabio Viviani

One of the reasons why I find my Country incredibly exciting when we begin to talk about food is because when you try to come up with the definition of what inspires the Italian Cuisine, and in particular, the cuisine coming from Florence, it is anything but easy. Every person that I know, every Grandmother that I've ever met, every single man or woman that has tried to teach me how to handle food properly gave me a different opinion about the nature of the cooking of my Country.

Our attachment to our roots is so remarkable that if you get in your car and drive one hour you will find a completely different reality when it comes to talking about food.

Everybody, though, is ready to recognize the sincerity and the equilibrium and the essence of our tradition in the kitchen, and how strong the bond is that ties our plate with our backyard, and the incredible product it has produced. But when it comes to saying aloud what is typical, which one is the plate that is the characteristic one from my hometown, which one is the cooking method that reigns supreme in my homeland, then that is when the idea becomes unclear and people start to argue with each other.

Some people think that everything that is characteristic of food from Florence should be fried: plates such as fried vegetables, fried lamb, fried chicken, fried anchovies, and fried pizza dough are a real must when it comes to having dinner in Florence. My Grandmother used to tell me, "If your grandmother fries them, even your old shoes are going to be good."

According to others, our tradition is based on grilling food: our grilled whole chicken, the remarkable steak, think about something that is walking in your backyard besides your dog or cat, doesn't matter if it is lamb, cow, duck, sheep, pig, it's going to taste AMAZING once you grill it. You're probably not going to like what I'm going to say, but in Italy, horse steak is a food that you find in Fine Dining Restaurants!

A 20-foot-long grill is easy to find when you go to the little villages of the countryside of Florence. The entire village gets together at certain times of the year and they roast or grill a huge amount of meat while they are using the oldest ingredient in the history of the food tradition: simplicity. If you talk to my family on the other side, everything should be braised or cooked in a tomato sauce: the eggs cooked in the oven with tomato sauce, the braised meat, the braised vegetables, our famous tomato bread soup, the chicken cacciatore, the tripe, the intestines cooked in tomato sauce and garlic, sausage and beans. Nothing that has been known to a human being, according to my mother, is going to taste bad if you braise it. And, as a chef, I can tell you, they are all right! The culinary traditions of my homeland are based on each and every one of these and some at the same time!

In this book, I'm going to tell you everything that I know about the reality that has been going on in my backyard in Florence. You may not like some of these things, but I didn't come to Moorpark to B***S*** you. We are going to tell you the truth, either you're going to like it or not. The difference between my way and the American way of dealing with food is huge. The first six months I was in this beautiful country, I was crying and pulling my hair out almost every night because the cultural difference between the way people deal with food here and back in my old Italy is so enormous. I was looking high and low for the same feeling about food. Nothing was the same. But I was here and I had to deal with it.

How many of you ever get up in the morning, put on muddy shoes and run downstairs to the backyard of your house to get the tomato right from the vine in order to get the sauce going on the late lunch? How many times have you seen the ocean from the pier in winter with your butt freezing while you are fishing for lobster or crab? How many times have you cleaned and gutted the fish in the sink on top of the waterwheel behind your house in order to bring something to the barbecue at your Grandmother's house?

How many times have you gone with your Grandfather looking for mushrooms? Getting up at 3:00 in the morning and driving for two hours to get there and two hours to get back in order to find 20 or 30 pounds of the best Porcini Mushrooms you have ever seen. Some were 4 or 5 pounds each. I can still remember the smell of them.

Did you ever get an infection in your finger because you got stuck with the spines of sea urchins that your were trying to pull from a rock in the seaside town where your Grandmother grew up? Did you ever try to eat a Mussel seasoned only with sea water because you are still at the water's edge, swimming close to the huge pillar where the mussels grow free in the ocean? I'm sure few, if any of you, have experienced these things, which have so impacted my way of dealing with food.

At the beginning of my American career, I was the chef in an Italian restaurant in Ventura, California, a cute little town right by the ocean. I was asking where we were buying the fish and sometime they would send me to the grocery store. This made my flesh creep! I was wondering how it was possible that we buy fish from the market or from some company that sends me fish that look old and tired instead of from a tank of a fishing boat at the pier. I was used to getting up at 3:00 in the morning to go to my local fish market and wait for the guys from the fishing boats that have been out all night catching fish. They come in around 3:30 AM with their catch and I'm used to dealing straight with the fishermen to get the freshest pieces.

Now I get to do this. Not like when I first moved here and I had to deal with some nasty fish that the restaurant owner was happy to buy because it was cheaper and shame on me if I was trying to get a better and fresher fish. The cost needs to be low in order to make money. I get that. But you also need to understand that customers are willing to pay more if the quality is good. If you have quality food, people will talk about how good the food is and your get more customers and respect than if you have mediocre food with mediocre ingredients.

Still, now some people complain that we serve an 8-9 ounce salmon steak for $24 and they tell me that at the chain restaurant close by they can get a Salmon combo with pasta and shrimp for $16.95. You know what? Go ahead and get your salmon at that place! Do you really think their salmon is the same? The same quality?

Do you know that you can find at least 10 different kinds of salmon in the restaurant business? The salmon that I get, I cannot charge $16 because it costs me $18 and is coming from some remote part of Alaska caught from a fishing boat by someone that doesn't even know that there are places in the world that raise salmon in a commercial pool, add color to the food to make the red flesh and hormones to make them bigger. You may not care, but I will continue to serve the best quality salmon I can buy to my customers for $24 and be proud of it.

In foods there are highs and lows. Why do you think the tomatoes you see in the grocery store all look the same? Because there is genetic modification that doesn't allow the plant to grow naturally.

A tomato that has been grown by a farmer on the two acres behind his farmhouse and watered every day by hand, every single plant baby-sat every day, each plant cleaned by hand, fertilized with mulch instead of sprays with chemicals...of course, they are bigger and they charge you more. And, it is worth it.

The other choice you have is to buy tomatoes that have been grown with hormones and they all look the same. They weight the same and they taste the same because they have been grown in 24 hours of light in a temperature controlled environment with no insects because the insects have been killed by the hormones! If birds and bugs are not comfortable eating your vegetables and fruits, maybe you shouldn't either!

A person gets up at 3:00 in the morning to go fishing or search for mushrooms or till the soil every day so in the month of August I can give you, just for two months, the best tasting tomato that God allows.

If I work 16 hours a day in order to create the best food possible; If I stay up all night to finish the fresh pasta recipe for you to taste the difference between a commercial pasta and my fresh pasta; or if I have to keep my meat in the refrigerator sitting for six weeks in order to give you the best dry-aged rib eye in the country; and if I try to give my whole heart and soul and all my passion to serve the very best that I can, then of course you pay more. It is called the "Price of Quality." The alternative is that you get up at 3:00 AM and go fishing or searching for mushrooms, you go and pick your tomatoes and then when you are exhausted, you also have to cook and clean. This may cost you less money, but you have worked you're a** off, or, you may go to a chain restaurant where you buy S*****food for less money, which will ruin your health, but you saved $10!

The solution is easy...let us cook for you. Let us take our passion and get up early to go to the market to get the best fish and the best cut of meat, the best vegetables, and work those 16 hours a day to produce the very best food. Let us cook and clean. You take care of your health through our good food and you will not only enjoy your dinner more, your will live longer and those extra $10 that you paid is worth it. We only want you to be healthy and happy!

Buon Appetito

My commitment to health for kids.....

All started from a dream and building kidshealthcafe.com has been a great pleasure for me. I have always envisioned my life being involved in one way or another with the betterment of children. After coming to the United States, one of the first things I noticed was how overweight many Americans are, especially children. Coming from Italy, it was a big shock for me because when you think of America you have an image of all things being good and healthy.

Unfortunately, since I've been here, I've seen many small children and teenagers with what I have heard called in America, "Muffin Top." In the food business, a muffin top is that extra batter that hangs over the side of a muffin. Of course, it looks good on a muffin, but not on children! In Italy, you don't see this so called muffin top on children. I know some people might think it's funny, but when you see children and teenagers that are overweight, it's no laughing matter. I really feel bad for these kids because most of them don't have a choice regarding the food they eat; they eat what their parents have taught them to eat. So, since I am a chef, I started thinking about what type of food is causing this syndrome. The longer I was here in the United States, the more I started to notice the availability and quantity of the crappy food that people are putting in their bodies. I hear stories of children with diabetes and heart disease, and after looking around, I can understand why. In my country grandparents, not kids, have these diseases. If I could be the voice of America, it would sound something like this: "Amore, you are killing your kids! Stop feeding them garbage!"

I visited the doctor maybe three or four times during my entire childhood. It seems like American children are visiting the doctor four to five times a year. I'm telling you, this is crazy! Although America might be the land of opportunity, maybe you have too much opportunity to stuff yourself with disgusting food. America does lead the world by example in many good ways, but when it comes to food choices, come on, and give me a break. The ready-made food available here sucks for the most part! You are poisoning your children with toxic processed foods. Have you ever taken a serious look at the ingredients in the prepackaged food you feed your children? The food choices you make as an adult are your business, but please don't make poor food choices for your kids. They deserve better!

I grew up on red meat, pasta, fresh fish, vegetables and fresh bread. I just had my cholesterol checked, and the doctor told me I was one of the healthiest people he has seen in a long time. Seriously, I can give you his number and you can call him himself! In Italian kitchens, you can't walk over to the cabinet and open a box of ready-to-eat snacks or food. When I was hungry after school, I would cut a piece of bread and rub it down with fresh tomato and garlic. Or, I'd make some pasta. Whatever the case, it was always fresh and I had to make it. I truly believe this is one reason why American children are unhealthy. Almost everything they eat comes from a box filled with preservatives and is artificial. Your body doesn't know how to process preservatives. But all is not lost, American parents. You can reverse the problem. Trust me, just start feeding your kids fresh food and you will see them blossom with good health.

I also strongly believe one of the reasons why American children are so unhealthy is because they don't exercise much. I don't mean they have to go the gym and sweat like a pig, but they do need to move. Most kids today come home from school and plop themselves down in front of the TV or play a video game. And that's it, as if they are petrified wood! It's OK to watch TV or play video games. I do it and, all modesty aside, I'm pretty good at it. But I don't sit for hours at a time. I can still hear my mom's voice saying, "Fabio, go outside and play. It's not healthy to sit around." I understand that Americans are very busy, but what's wrong with encouraging your kids to move around more and be more physical? You only get one body, and you need to take care of it!

Because of all this, I started kidshealthcafe.com. I wanted to offer my experience of Italian culture and my knowledge through food to help parents and children become informed and make better food choices. I want to be the "Muffin Slayer" of America!

I believe kidshealthcafe.com offers some of the best health and wellness resources available online. Our leadership team includes professionals such as doctors, chiropractors, dieticians, holistic wellness practitioners, personal trainers, educators, licensed family therapists, acupuncturists, massage therapists and other wellness-oriented experts (not to mention an incredible chef with great healthy recipes!). Kidshealthcafe.com is committed to be the number one resource for everyone interested in improving and maintaining their children's health, nutrition, and general wellness. We are developing a strong wellness community utilizing live forums where qualified health professionals will respond to your questions. Kidshealthcafe.com is developing a partnership with local school districts and large brand name food manufacturers to help bring awareness to families and support a healthier nutrient-rich life. Our interactive social community will allow parents and families to stay connected and informed on topics that are important to their developing children.

We are committed to providing a broad array of ways for parents to learn and connect with each other as we all work toward building a generation of children with healthy bodies and minds and well-balanced diets and lives.

Please visit my website today. Registration is free. Please help me to help kids, there are too many of them in this country; it's impossible for me do it by myself. Children are such a gift. Please help me create a better future for them. If you don't visit my Website and register, I will have to call the Food-Police and have them bring you in Jail.

__Fabio Viviani

What is it about our work that makes us who we are? I sometimes think about how a person spends their day. All of the little things they do with their mind, with their body, with their hands. I wonder this as I experiment in the kitchen developing new garnishes and service styles and I see my hands working in a way that I am familiar with. I love my craft. I love being able to have the freedom to create with my hands.

Sometimes I catch myself daydreaming while I'm looking at my hands and wonder about the lives of others. I'm Italian, so obviously in addition to using my hands for work; I can't seem to talk without them!

In my chosen path in life, I rely on my hands like a sculptor uses his. My hands, like my bar kit, are my tools. As I run my fingers along the edge of the locks on my little case, I notice for the first time that two of the corners of my case are fraying a little bit on one end. For some reason, until this moment it had not occurred to me that I will have this case for the rest of my life. Inside are the many tools I have collected over the years of my life's work. Each one has its own story, life and purpose. Some of them have undergone transformations, some have been passed down to me, some I have made myself, and some of them even have a name. I'm sure they're worthless in value, but each of these instruments is priceless to me. Like a pen to a poet, like brushes to an artist; these are the tools of my trade.

Can something as simple as lemon and oranges transformed into fish? What about turning a zucchini into a tulip? Or what about a watermelon that becomes lover's first kiss? Not only is it possible, but it's really cool and always seems to make a serious impression! There are a lot of different ideas that can bring a new and special touch to your Martini. A butternut squash that becomes a Fleur d' Les. Even a honeydew melon shaped as the Florence skyline, with an apple sliced like stars.

You will love this section; it will give you the chance to impress your friends and loved ones. Not only should this section expand your knowledge of mixology, but also your hidden artistic skill that will make the experience of learning garnish art all the more memorable for you.

It will be not so difficult to give a total personal touch to your drink if using a curving knife (or any simple knife) and a few little secrets that I'm going to help you discover in this book! The garnish art of fruits and vegetables has always been a secret art which has been closely kept from the public by all the big chefs. I think its time to show them to everyone! This will be in other words, a section focused on the "art of the cut" and of the art of the garnish itself.

So, my friends! As we begin, keep that knife in your hand, express all the art that is in you, and follow my little tips. Never forget: what pleases the eye pleases the palate.

This part of the book will give you an experience in Garnish Art.

Butternut squash, potato, taro root, melon, watermelon, dikon...the list of fruit and vegetables used to create garnitures is longer than you can imagine. There are actually a few suggestions to follow to acquire the right product. It is better to select fruit and vegetables that are in season; they are easier to cut and carve and are less expensive. All of them need to be firm and the skin must look impeccable. Usually, the leaves are the sign of freshness, especially for carrots and radishes. Regarding the butternut squash, you can hold onto them for months if kept in a dry place. The melon and the watermelon are easier to carve when they are not ripe. What is the secret to knowing which one to buy? Buy the one that doesn't have a scent. And watermelons are two different colors; one with a dark skin is easy to find from April to May and the light is available in June.

Step by Step

It is surprising to see for the first time a butternut squash become a fleur-de-lis or an orange became a chrysanthemum. It is a little magic that everybody can do. To learn doesn't require extreme patience, only a little of attention and a little handy technique. In the step by step explanation, all the instructions are described and shown in detail. Is forbidden be discouraged. To start getting some practice, it's better start with the easier garnitures like the chamomile flowers or the orange knot.

Always clean and dry the fruit and the vegetables well before used. You can prepare the garniture beforehand. Potatoes, carrots and radishes are easy to store. They can be stored in the refrigerator for a few days in water. Iced water will ruin the radish, however, it will be perfect for the onions and leek flower garnitures. For carrots, potatoes, red and white beets and zucchini, it is important to use mineral water with the addition of 1-2% pure alcohol (90 proof). The alcohol can be easily found at the supermarket. The watermelon, once carved, can be stored in the refrigerator for several hours. It will be best to wrap them in several layers of wet paper towels or a wet kitchen towel. If the watermelon will be eaten, make sure that the kitchen towel you use has not been washed in any strong detergent because this will change the taste of the fruit. The melon, after being carved and before placing in the refrigerator, must be wrapped in wet paper towels and then covered with plastic wrap. Apples, pears and eggplants look like they have been freshly cut if they are sprinkled with lemon juice, which can be applied with a small brush or using a spray bottle. The lemon juice must be filtered so it does not have pulp or seeds and diluted with water. After using the skins, never throw away the remaining fruit. It will make a great fruit salad. The same goes for your vegetables. They will make great minestrone!

There are only two ways to live your life. One is as though nothing is a miracle. The other is as if everything is.

__ Albert Einstein

Attrezzi Del Mestiere (Bar Tools)

Now, I hope you're not thinking that you can simply use your kitchen cup and silverware to mix, stir, and shake excellent Martinis, are you? After all, the difference between ordinary and amazing can often be the result of just a little extra attention to detail. Don't worry though, making beautiful drinks is fun, entertaining, and always worth the effort. So, with a little research and a little extra money, you'll be ready to go - Bartender style!

Ten pieces of equipment is all you will need to put together a "cocktail kit" worthy of its title. Remember: Use of an appropriate instrument is a requirement if you want to succeed in your objective. Cocktail Martinis, specifically, deserve this level of care and attention! Since making the most incredible drinks your friends have ever had is your objective, once you have acquired your cocktail kit your can start working.

Some time has passed since Tom Cruise was preparing cocktails in a movie that brought passion to the profession of bartending. Obviously, the visuals in the movie made everyone want to flip bottles around and make six drinks at once. By the way, I have my own array of acrobatic tricks, and sometimes it is fun to show off over in the Martini Lounge of our beloved Café Firenze. But the truth is that the real quality of the drink, and in fact the true study of Mixology, has nothing to do with flare or bottle-spinning or bar tricks. To really get it right, you will need the right instruments, instruction, and ingredients.

So, now that I've totally gone overboard explaining the delicate nature of the task at hand, let's all get to work and start having some fun!

Bar Kit:

These pieces of equipment are needed to put together a noteworthy cocktail. It is not a matter of show. The use of the appropriate instrument is essential if you want to create a cocktail martini that deserves all our attention! Once you complete your kit you can start working!

Decoration Tong: These also are called fruit tongs and should be in stainless steel to guarantee the maximum longevity. Good for grabbing items such as cherries, sugar cubes, and fruits for all the special cocktail garnitures.

Ice Spoon: You can find different shapes and materials with the most common being stainless steel. However, you can find them also in transparent or colored polycarbonate; some look just like a big scoop and others look like bigger tablespoons with holes to let the water drip.

Mixing Spoon: This is a crucial instrument for a good bartender. It is needed to chill the mixing glass before pouring the ingredients and to mix all those cocktail that don't need to be shaken. The Cocktail martini is the number one cocktail in the USA. It is not supposed to be shaken because if you do it, the vermouth changes characteristics. Going back to our beautiful mixing spoon, it is longer that any other spoon and the handle part is made as a spiral to rotate between the fingers. On one extremity of the handle is attached a sort of little circle that is used as a muddler. You should never set a functional workstation without one!

Strainer: Italian bartender will say, "What? Stranger? Is called Colino!" It is a force filter that is used to filter the ice from the drink. It is used with the Boston shaker.

Boston Shaker: This tool has completely destroyed the use of the impractical continental style shaker since it is easier and faster to prepare varied quantities of drinks. It is made of two parts: one in stainless steel and one in glass. The most modern one can be personalized with the name of the bartender or the bar. We can find on the market different colors that are waterproof also.

MIKE, FABIO & JACOPO

ANTIPASTI - APPETIZER

APPETIZERS

In my country there is not a typical dish that you eat when you're hungry or when you sit down at the table. It never happens that a friend of mine tells me "let's go have a salad" or "today, I want pasta."

Every meal has many components and it doesn't matter if you have 10 minutes or the whole evening, you have to respect the harmony and order of the meal. That is why we don't serve the meat with the potato on the same plate. The potato will come right after because it is a 'Contorni', a side dish that will complete the main course rather than challenge it. Salad is a side dish. You do not eat a salad as a main course. We don't have smaller salads and entrée salad portions...we have a salad. That is it.

Same thing for the antipasto; antipasto is a slice of cold cut or piece of vegetable perfectly grilled or a slice of the best cheese of the town you are in, or even simpler, three filet of anchovies with bread and butter.

The appetizer in this country is more refined, more complete. More than one or two components can be found on your starter and this is a dish on its own. This is not what we call Antipasto. In Italy, antipasto means 'before the meal'. For us it is thousands of single things presented to you one after the other while your wait for the actual meal.

I have tried to keep the recipes simple as I do when I am presenting them myself and in a way that is appealing to you. For us, antipasto is a combination of lots of little things rather than a single portion of something. But it is also true that many times when you are having lunch or dinner with my Mom, after the antipasto you are so full that you don't feel like eating anymore...until the next glass of wine.

Of course you're full. You've not been drinking. Here, have another glass of wine that is very good for your blood (that is what my Grandpa would say)...and another glass of wine and by and by you realize what is happening...you are full, you are drunk, but you are happy and ready to start your meal.

__Fabio

CARPACCIO DI TONNO

Miso Dressing and Butter poached Asparagus, Crushed Black Peppercorn and Chive
4 servings

FOR THE TUNA:

4 Tuna steaks about 4 oz each.
The tuna that you want to use for this plate is something that is a good choice if eaten raw, so you will have to stick with either Pacific Bluefin (the Atlantic Bluefin is almost extinct - don't eat that please), which is the most expensive and tasty because has higher fat content, the good fat, or you can choose the yellow fin, which is good as well but less refined. The other thing good about Yellowfin is that it is the most prolific species in the entire tuna dynasty and the species is not at risk of extinction. I will stay away from Albacore and if you want know why go in the box at the end of the recipe.

Whole black Peppercorn - about 4 tsp
4 Tsp of Fleur de Sel or a good Flaky Salt
Fleur de Sel can be find in any well-furnished food market and the reason why you should use this type of salt, especially if there is no need to cook the protein that are you using, is because it is a hand-harvested sea salt that has been collected by workers who scrap only the top layer of salt before it sinks to the bottom of large salt pans. The result is a tastier salt, with full flavour but yet not too strong and still naturally moist from the ocean water. Don't get me wrong, I mean...you can use regular table salt as well and probably will be useful for the purpose, but if you use the right ingredient you will have a totally different experience – it is like go and have a ride with a huge motorbike, or use a skateboard instead, you probably still get wherever you want but the whole experience will change...I'll go with the motorbike.

1 Bunch of Chive
A Bottle of Extra Virgin Olive Oil
Place two sheets of plastic wrap one on top of the other, and put one of the tuna steaks in the middle. Place on top of the fish 2 more sheets of plastic wrap. Start pounding the fish with a meat mallet. Don't pound too strongly or the meat will smash. Little by little you have to shape the tuna steak 1/8 of an inch thick. Using a knife, cut the edge of the tuna and make it look like a square, season now with crushed black peppercorn, a sprinkle of Fleur de Sel and some chopped Chives, drizzle with extra virgin olive oil.

FOR THE MISO:

4 oz of Red or white Miso paste
Miso is a typical Japanese traditional paste made out of the fermentation process of soybean, rice and barley with the addition of sea salt and kojikin, which just for the sake of the knowledge is a fungus that helps the fermentation process. You have to use this kind of paste just because the aroma and flavor typical of the miso paste is perfect with the delicate flavor of the tuna. You can find miso paste in any Asian market or in a good food market. If you don't trust using ingredients that you don't know or if you don't like miso (that is a possibility) you can use simply some squeezed lemon juice. Another thing to know is also that there is no big difference between red and white miso paste. I know that Miso is not quite Italian, but you can stretch the rules sometime – just don't tell my grandma!

2 Tbsp. of fresh Lemon Juice
¾ C of Mineral water
1 pinch of Hungarian Paprika: Paprika is a spice made from the grinding of dried sweet red or green bell peppers. The Hungarian type is the most common also because "Paprike" means Peppers in Hungarian Language. You can find this item easily in any food store. I prefer the Hungarian because has a sweeter flavor and more spiciness in respect to any other paprika.

1 pinch of Fresh chopped Parsley

FOR THE ASPARAGUS:

16 Asparagus medium size
1 stick of Butter
Salt and fresh ground Black Pepper
3 Cloves of Garlic

Melt the butter in a saucepan over medium/high fire, peel and press the garlic clove with the blade of your knife, and let the garlic cook in the butter at low fire. Add the asparagus raw, peeled just from the half toward the end part and sliced in half lengthwise. The fire has to be on low, keep the asparagus as long as you like for the texture (but not less than 8-10 minutes), take them out and add the crushed pepper, save the brown butter for drizzle on the tuna.

REASON WHY I WILL NOT EAT ALBACORE TUNA:

Albacore is a fish but it doesn't know it is. It will drown if stops swimming. Now, you know no fish can really drown, well the Albacore can.

Unlike other species of fish, in order to be alive it has to keep swimming without stopping for the whole length of his life, swimming brings oxygen-filled water in their gills and allows them to breath, and they need to swim as much as they can because their body needs a lot of oxygen. Albacore is a really strong fish.

It is a worldwide fish, you can find it in every ocean: Indian, Pacific, Atlantic and sometimes also in the Mediterranean Sea but just if he get lost partying out of the coast of Ibiza. It is really a great fish and spends the biggest part of his life in open ocean, away from pollution. It goes back and forward from North America coast to the coast of Japan where it breeds a bunch of little baby tuna, that as soon they can have a passport, they go to North America again to date some other tuna and start the process all over again. It is really a high migratory species.

The younger the fish is (2 to 4 years), the closer it swims toward the surface of the ocean and the better and healthier the fish is. Rich in Omega-3 acid, this is the best time of his life to be eaten by us but the problem is 95% of the fish caught are too young (1 to 2 years old) to deserve to be in the plate of somebody. Professional fisherman keep their net on the surface of the ocean in order to try to catch the younger tuna. The older fish (5 years and up) are almost never caught because they swim in really deep water. They also are not that great in taste, so either you have to choose to kill a very young albacore, or eat a not-so-great piece of fish. Honestly, I'm not looking for any of that. I try to support sustainable fish catch and treat animals well so my little world does not support this. That's all.

Don’t be sadish, have a radish!
__Anonymous

COCKTAIL MARTINI

2 ¾ oz (11counts) Gin/Vodka
¼ oz (1count) Dry Vermouth

1 Bleu Cheese Stuffed Olive
1 Radish
2 cloves

PREPARATION: We prepare this drink in a mixing glass with ice. DO NOT shake it! Never shake vermouth or it will loose the unique aroma! Squeeze a lemon peel on the surface so that the essential oils come out and give a nice refreshing aftertaste. Serve in a chilled Martini glass with olives...Well, if you really want to be fancy, do it like we do it, stick your stem-less martini glass in a glass full of ice water to keep the martini cold and to keep the garnish nice and fresh!

The drink must look as crisp as possible to give an immediate sense of refreshment. The nose is of rich herbs and spices and the mouth is an explosion of strong flavors. As we say, you'll love it or you'll hate it!

These characteristics make it this perfect for Tuna Carpaccio.

LA STORIA: We say this famous cocktail was born in 1910 at the Knickerbocker where Mr. Martini, an Italian Dude, was working. Of course, I was going to say he was Italian even if he was from Morocco!

He decided to modify the Gin and French cocktail classic drink made from equal parts Gin and French Vermouth. Mister Martini used the same ingredients but changed the portions (11 parts to 1 Part) and the preparation (he mixed them and poured them in a glass with not a single cube of ice) which gave birth to one of, if not the most famous, mixed drinks ever made!

Well, he did make a substantial change to the recipe. He replaced the French Vermouth with Italian Vermouth (and with this I've said everything! Of course it was better...it was Italian!) which gave the final result a drier taste...the trend and the evolution of the drinkers is bringing the recipe to be always drier and drier until now, a lot of them drink it with no vermouth at all!

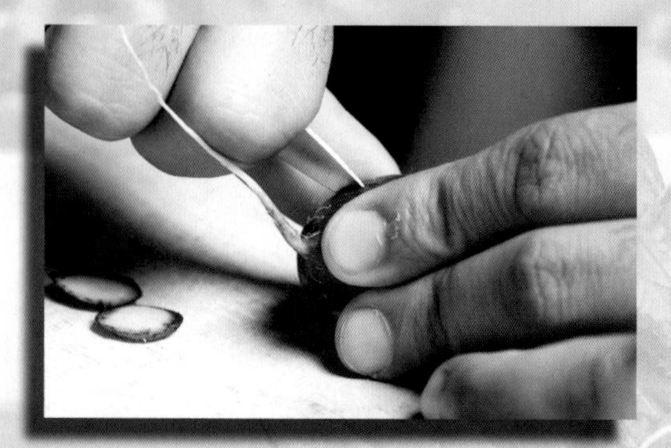

Using a small radish, we take our "spelucchino"(paring) knife and make two adjacent cuts across the lower half, away from the "tail," creating two white, circular surfaces which will be the eyes of the mouse.

Using the two white circular discs created in step one, place them above the eyes by making two small incisions directly above, towards the "tail," each "eye."

Take two cloves, and insert the stem deep into the "eye" circles to give life to our radish mouse. Make a final third incision, opposite the "ears," so our "mouse" has a place to sit on our martini glass.

Insert a nice toothpick or garnish pick into the "mouth" (the small protruding portion of the radish below the eyes) pushing it all the way through, leaving only about a half inch sticking out the mouth so we can place our bleu cheese stuffed olive at the end.

Life is like a box of chocolates, you never know what you're gonna get...so that's why we eat steak!
__Jacopo & Fabio

CARPACCIO DI MANZO:
Beef Carpaccio, Roasted Mushrooms, Shaved Parmesan and Lemon Vinaigrette
4 servings

FOR THE CARPACCIO:
1.5 lbs. of Prime Beef Tenderloin
1 Tsp of Fleur de Sel
1 Tsp of Black Crushed Peppercorn

Clean the Tenderloin and remove fat and silver skin. Using the plastic wrap, tie the meat in a form of a cylinder and place in the freezer for at least 4 hours. Once almost frozen, slice the meat using a really sharp knife or a home slicer. For the thickness I wouldn't go more than 1/8 of an inch. Season with crushed pepper and Fleur de Sel.

FOR THE ROASTED MUSHROOMS:
8 oz Chanterelle mushrooms
8 oz Hen of Wood mushrooms
Or Maitaki, they can be easily found in any well-stocked food store. I love them because they have a salty flavor and a really meaty texture, and I like to combine them with the other 2 kinds of mushrooms in this recipe, very common in Europe and Asia. This mushroom can grow to reach 60 pounds (a must-have if you are a mushroom lover).

8 oz Lobster mushrooms
The word Lobster is not, in the truest sense of the word, referring to the actual mushroom. We are talking about a good parasitic spore that grows on mushrooms, turning them a red-orange color that resembles the shell of a cooked lobster. Lobster mushrooms are widely eaten and enjoyed; they are commercially marketed and are commonly found in some large grocery stores. They have a seafood-like flavor and a firm, dense texture.

3 sprigs of Thyme
8 cloves of Garlic
1 sprig of Rosemary
Kosher Salt
Crushed Black Peppercorn
1 lb of Butter

Clean the dirt from the mushrooms at the bottom and cut them in 3-4 pieces each, blanch them in boiling water, separating them for type. Each mushroom has a different timing of blanching and you can feel it from touching the head and the steam - if spongy will blanch faster - if firm will take more time because it won't absorb water as fast as the other one. Once done set them in a dry towel. Melt half of the butter with the thyme inside and the crushed garlic and the rosemary, let the butter and Herbs go for 6-8 minutes on medium fire. Add the mushrooms and bring the fire to high. When the edges of the mushrooms are getting a nice brown color it is time to turn the fire off. Strain the butter (you can keep it to flavor other dishes). Discard the herbs and most of the garlic, add salt and fresh crushed pepper to the mushrooms and let them cool down, if you like you can drizzle them with a good extra virgin olive oil.

FOR THE LEMON VINAIGRETTE:

3 Meyer Lemons

The Meyer lemon is fruit, native to Orient; it is a cross between a lemon and a mandarin orange. It is yellow and rounder than a true lemon with a slight orange tint when ripe. It has a sweeter, less acidic flavor and a fragrant edible skin, which personally I love, at its best if cut in half and grilled right before using it.

½ Cup Olive Oil

Squeeze the lemon making sure that the seeds are discarded, strain the lemon juice so you won't have the pulp inside and mix the lemon juice with the olive oil, shake well or use a blender.

FOR THE SHAVED PARMESAN:

8 oz of Aged Parmesan cheese

Using a Potato peeler, shave the parmesan paper thin and add some on top of the Carpaccio.

Gli italiani hanno solo due cose per la testa: L` altra sono gli spaghetti!

The Italian has only two things on his mind – the other one is spaghetti!

MOJITALIAN
1 ½ oz. (6 counts) Light Rum
½ oz (2 counts) Amaretto Disaronno
1 rosemary sprig
3 lime wedge (½ lime)
1 ½ teaspoons of brown or white granulated sugar
½ oz soda water

1 Watermelon

PREPARATION:

Take three lime wedges and place them with one and a half teaspoons of brown sugar. Once you've tried this, you can adjust the amount of sugar depending on how sweet you like your drinks. This kind of sugar can be found in the market in different varieties, but the best result will be from brown sugar crystal. Add the rosemary and muddle to bring the entire aroma out of your spices. You should now have a juice with a greenish color in your glass, take a nice smell! We're half way there! Continue by adding the ounce and a half of light rum and finish by adding a half ounce of the #1 Italian liquor, Amaretto Disaronno. Shake it hard with ice to release even more flavor, and serve it in a long drink glass filled with crushed ice.

The color is a sexy light green with dark green veins; the perfume is strongly dominated by the rosemary. The drink is pretty thick, almost oily, but very tasty and well-balanced.

LA STORIA:

This is a variation of one of the most consumed cocktails ever made, the Moijto. We say that by 1600, the famous pirate Sir Francis Drake was drinking it with his troops while crossing the Caribbean Sea. Once the natives of the land took the first sip, a non-stop party began which didn't stop for over two hundred years. Later on, during the 1950s and 60s it was a big trend in all the summer Caribbean resorts. The Mojito was a favorite drink for the famous author Ernest Hemingway. Receipts show that he had the bartenders prepare his moijtos at the Boteguita del Medio in 1942 in Havana.

Now, by adding the famous spirit of the Italian culture, Amaretto Disaronno and the popular Italian spice rosemary, we create an amazing twist on this historic favorite that is sure to be a trend for the new era of the Mojito lover!

Take a large watermelon and using a large kitchen knife, cut a thin, long slice of the skin to create our "watermelon canvas".

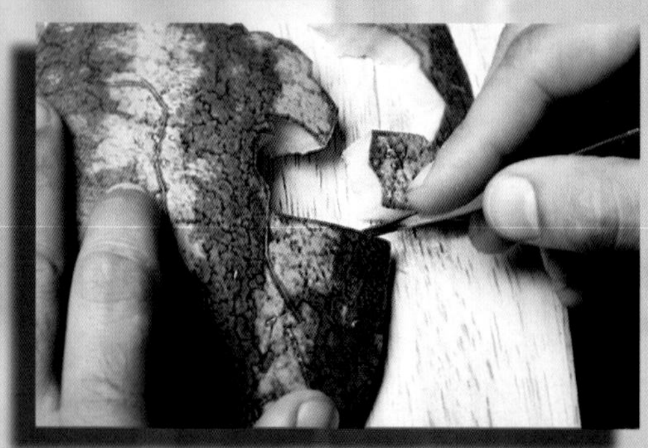

Using a stencil of the greatest country in the world, guide a small knife tip along the edge of the stencil to create an outline of my country, and begin to cut!

Making sure to cut from the outline in quarters of the design, will give you plenty of room to work with your canvas.

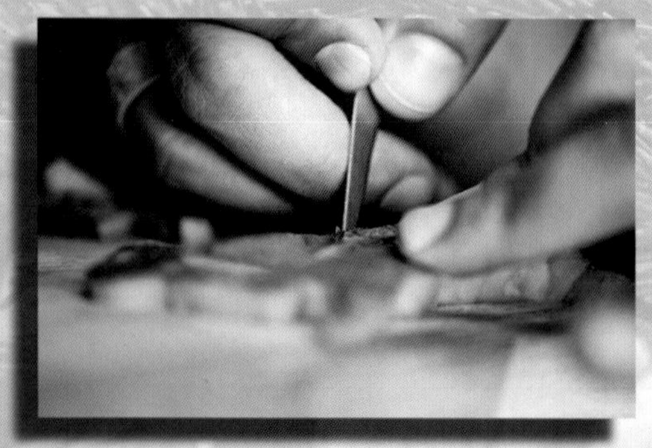

After the cut-out is complete, make a small incision from the coast of Toscana to the greatest city in the world (Firenze), to give our country a proper niche to rest on the glass.

There are artists who depict the sun as a yellow spot – but there are others that thanks to their art, transform the yellow spot into the sun!

__Pablo Picasso

GNOCCHI FRITTI:

Fried Potato Gnocchi Black truffle Gorgonzola sauce, fresh Pears and Prosciutto di Parma
4 servings

FOR THE POTATO GNOCCHI:

5 Medium size Russet or Kennebec Potatoes
You want to use this kind of potato because they have less content in starch. If the only potato that you have is IDAHO or BAKING in your pantry and you are maybe lazy and you don't want to go to the grocery store in order to buy a different potato because it's easier use what you have already in your house; well you maybe want to know that if the food-police will get to know what you've done, you may go in Jail for several years. I'm Italian listen to me; you really need the right potato to do the gnocchi unless you want them hard like a rock. Gnocchi have to be fluffy and moist, not hard and chewy, and if you still don't want listen to me I hope that the food-police will come and get you.

1 Nutmeg 6 oz of Parmesan Cheese
½ Tsp of Fresh Ground Black Pepper
1 Large Egg (or 2 smaller)
1 Tsp of Table Salt
8 oz of Regular Flour plus some for dust
1 Stick of Butter

Peel the potatoes and boil them in water. They have to be cooked but still firm. You will be able when done to cut through with a butter knife but still find some resistance in the consistency of the potato. Put them in the mixer with the paddle attachment and add the melted butter, the eggs, the salt and pepper and the nutmeg, grated with a micro plane (which is a special grater for dry nuts, very commonly used in pastry preparation, and easy to find in any kitchen store). Mix on high speed in order to break down the potato, scrape the edge of the mixer and mix again.

Spread the mixture in flat sheet pans and refrigerate overnight. The next day the potato has lost part of the moisture, place them again in the mixer with the paddle attachment and incorporate the flour, adding in 3 separate increments.

Keep mixing for another 5 minutes once the flour is all added. Remove the dough from the mixer and cut the dough in smaller pieces. You should be able to roll them and make snake-like shapes pieces of dough. Dust with flour and cut the gnocchi in ½ inch by ½ inch size. Place them in a refrigerator. When ready, fry them in hot oil (350 degrees) till golden brown.

FOR THE BLACK TRUFFLE GORGONZOLA SAUCE:

8 oz of Italian Creamy Gorgonzola
1 Black Summer Truffle (canned if not Fresh)
1 Tsp Fresh crushed Black Pepper
½ Cup of Heavy Cream
1 Tbsp of good Truffle Olive Oil

Set the Gorgonzola out of the refrigerator because you need that at room temperature. Bring the heavy cream to boil on low fire, add the gorgonzola and transfer to a bowl, stirring till the cheese is melted in the cream. If too liquid, return to fire again on low and keep stirring.
Add the pepper and the truffle oil. Shave the truffle with a truffle slicer or grate it with a microplane. Let rest for couple of minutes. Drizzle around the plate.

FOR THE SLICED PEAR AND PROSCIUTTO:

2 Bosch Pear (or any kind of Firm Flesh Pear)
1 Lb of Parma Prosciutto thinly sliced

Cut the pear in half and in half again (lengthwise), discard the seeds and slice smaller sections thin, place the Pear in the center surrounded with the Prosciutto and the Fried Gnocchi, drizzle with the sauce.

Yesterday is history, tomorrow a mystery,
but today is a gift, that is why it is called the present.
__Anonymous

PEAR TINI

1 ¼ oz (5 counts) Pear Vodka
1 oz (4 counts) Fresh pear nectar
½ oz (2 counts) Homemade sweet and sour
¼ oz (1 count) Triple sec
1 Lime Wedge (squeezed)

One Bosc Pear
One Cantaloupe Melon
Cinnamon powder
White Sugar

PREPARATION: Grab the mixing glass and pour 1 ¼ oz of infused pear vodka then 1 oz of pear nectar. Make sure it is nectar and not juice otherwise your drink will be runny and flavorless instead of smooth and slick. Now add ½ oz of sweet and sour (see glossary). For the drink to have the best result it has to be made with the best products! This being said, would you ever use anything that is not fresh fruit?
Shake it and poor it in a chilled and sugar/cinnamon rimmed martini glass and... Salute!

The color is pale yellow, almost white with green reflections. The body is big for the thickness of the pear pulp. It has an intense flavor of pear, lemon and sugar that are easy to distinguish in the mouth and they blend together giving a fresh taste, a little alcoholic and astringent. A perfect summery drink to enjoy under the sun in a pool chair!

LA STORIA: My challenge is to make my martini a perfect social drink that can be paired with the amazing Fabio's creations. Now it is pretty complex to find aromas, tastes, and sensations that can make a savory plate perfectly paired to a Martini! The idea is always to have at least one or more of the ingredients of the food recipe in the drink and have tied them together! What can be better paired to a nice Appetizer truffle based served with fresh pear?

This is how we gave birth to this martini.

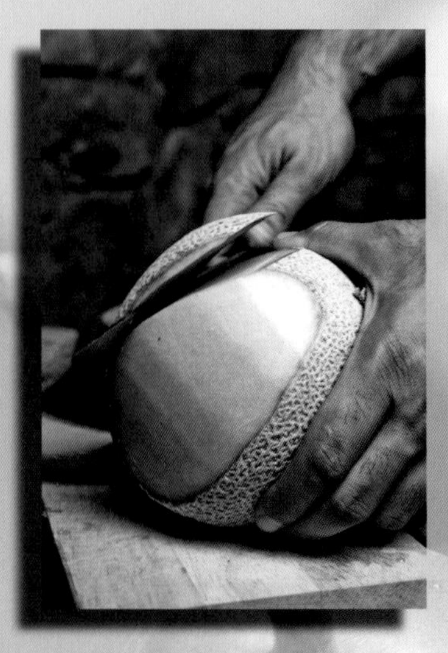

Take a cantaloupe melon, and cut a long thin piece of the skin away giving us a "melon canvas" to create our "worm."

Shape the worm by making a wave or "S" like pattern approximately 4 inches in length, remembering to shape the end of the head and tail.

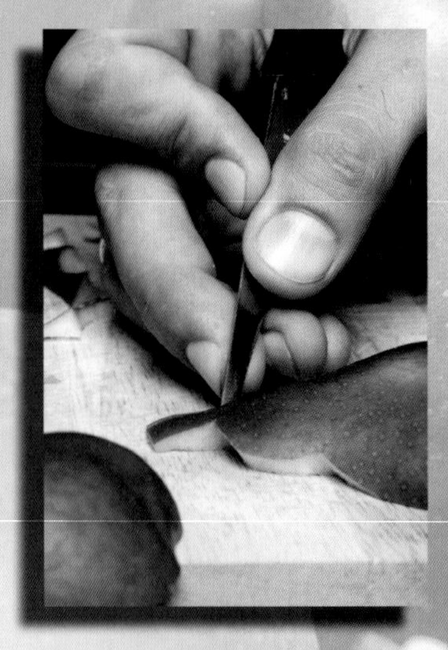

Now take a bosc pear (the pear that most resembles the stereotypical "pear" shape) and slice it vertically giving you a pear shaped segment. Now, using your paring knife, re-shape the top of the segment to re-semble the top and stem of the pear.

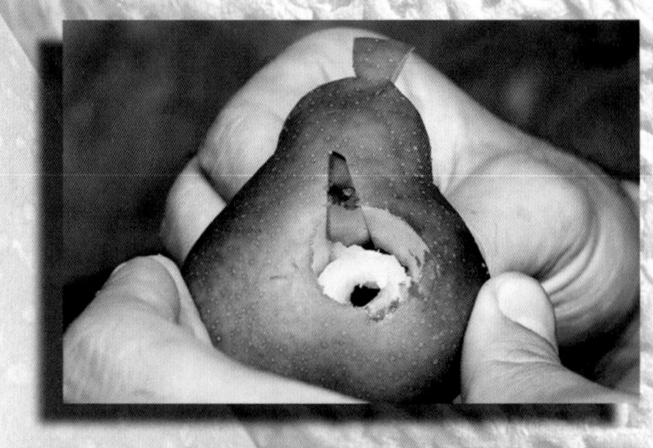

Carve a hole approximately the size of the tip of your finger in the lower right end of the "pear." Make sure the hole is large enough for our "melon worm" to fit into comfortably.

Insert the worm through the hole, and make an incision on the lower left side to give our pear and worm a place to sit on the rim of the martini glass.

A good friendship is like a good wine –
It only gets better with age!

GAMBERONI IN CAMICIA:

Pancetta wrapped Jumbo Prawn filled with Italian Sharp Gorgonzola with Parmesan Polenta
4 servings

FOR THE JUMBO PRAWN:

4 Jumbo Prawns

When I'm talking about Prawn, even knowing that there is a physical difference between an actual Prawn and a regular shrimp. I'm referring to a big size shrimp. Ask your fish guy to give you shrimp pretty big. A good size is when in a pound of shrimp you only count 6-8. This size is meatier and to me they taste better for this purpose.

4 oz Crumbled Sharp Gorgonzola
Fresh ground Pepper
½ C of Corn Syrup
8 oz of thinly sliced Italian Pancetta
½ C of Balsamic Vinegar

Peel the shell of the prawns and take the head off but leave the tail on. De-vein them and cut open the back with a sharp knife. Make a cut from the head to the tail. Season with fresh ground pepper on both sides.

Using the palm of your hand, press some of the crumbled Gorgonzola and shape it like a little bug. It has to fit in the opening in the back of the prawns. Close the lips of the meat around the shrimp and press them in the way that the Gorgonzola will stay.

If you noticed, the slice of pancetta is wrapping around itself. You can unwrap the pancetta and have one long strip for each slice. Starting from the tail of the prawn, wrap the pancetta around the whole body finishing with the head side, press the prawn by closing your hand around it so the pancetta will stick to the body. Set aside in the refrigerator.

Place the balsamic in a sauce pan and reduce to half, add the corn syrup and keep cooking for another 5 minutes, turn it down and let cool. Now you have your balsamic glaze.

Grill the shrimp till you have a nice crispy pancetta around, then if you like them more cooked you can finish in the oven at 400 for another 4 minutes, but I don't suggest that. I like my shrimp still little bit underdone in the very center.

FOR THE BABY SPINACH:

1 Lb of fresh baby spinach (the baby spinach has more tender leaf than a regular spinach)
3 Cloves of Garlic smashed with the side of a Knife (once cooked you can remove them)
Salt and fresh Ground Pepper
2 Tbsp of Extra Virgin Olive Oil

Heat the oil and add the garlic till golden brown (3-4 minutes), add the spinach and stir till they are wilted but not completely mushy (5 minutes), add salt & Pepper and set aside, heat them up again right before serving.

FOR THE POLENTA:

1 C of Polenta or Grits
1 C of Milk
1 C of Heavy Cream or for food allergies substitute Milk and Cream with 2 cups of Water
2 Cloves of Garlic very thinly sliced
Fresh Herbs chopped (Rosemary, Sage) about 1 Tbsp
Salt and Pepper
4 oz of grated Parmesan cheese
½ stick of butter (if you have allergies to Milk avoid this also)

Let the Herbs go with the butter for about 5-6 minutes, add the Milk and the Cream and bring to simmer, add the Polenta (or Grits) and bring the fire to low. Stir till you have a creamy but firm texture; add the Parmesan and season to taste with salt and pepper.

For the plating either see the picture or be little creative, come on...is not that hard!

Love rules without rules.
__Italian Proverb

BALSAMIC MARTINI

1 ½ oz (6 counts) Vanilla Rum
¾ oz (3 counts) Simple Syrup
½ oz (2 counts) Strawberry Puree
3 Small Strawberries
4 lime wedges
12-15 Dashes of Aged Balsamic Vinegar
1 Spaghetti Squash
Balsamic Glaze

PREPARATION:

Take three strawberries, make sure they are nicely washed and the stem is removed. Place them in the mixing glass and add a lime wedge and the ¾ oz of simple syrup (see glossary), 12/15 dashes of Balsamic Vinegar and ½ oz of the homemade simple syrup and start muddling. The muddling process is done while you are pressing the lime so the unique flavor of the essential oil contained in the skin comes out. Be careful to not over do it because it will result in bitter Minestrone!

Now we have a nice puree...but, where is the alcohol? Here it is! Rum! Add 1 ½ oz and it is time to fill the shaker with ice. Then, pour the mix into the shaker and start shaking! Strain into a balsamic glaze drizzled martini glass.

Burgundy color with amber rifles done from the balsamic glaze drizzled in the glass - has a clear perfume of Vanilla and pretty strong acidity notes. We are talking about a great refreshing drink due to the presence of lime, sugar, and balsamic vinegar very well balanced together. A beautiful clean and unusual aftertaste that lives your mouth ready for the next sip!

LA STORIA: My bar manager, Pauline Bonamigo and I wanted to create something very unique. I step into the kitchen and I started pulling out garlic, rosemary, basil, truffle, tomato...the weirdest things were flying out of the refrigerator! I started smelling them while I was looking on the bottle shelves for inspiration but nothing was coming to me! Until I noticed that the olive oil and the balsamic vinegar dispensers were not completely full and clean as I like. Before I could point this out to the one in charge, the light bulb turned on in my brain! Balsamic vinegar! Wow, this will be perfect! Italian restaurants must have a drink with balsamic vinegar, what do you think?

I start grabbing fruit...strawberries, of course! The best marriage for fruit and Balsamic is strawberries. I start thinking of some gelato or dessert recipes with those two ingredients so Pauline tells me lime! And, I think Panna cotta! I start muddling the strawberries; Pauline throws in a couple of limes and the balsamic. I grabbed the vanilla vodka but by mistake take the vanilla rum instead...I look at it for a second and I thought, why not? I started pouring. When I smelled it, I could tell that something special was happening. Yes! That was the first creation of the signature Café Firenze drinks!

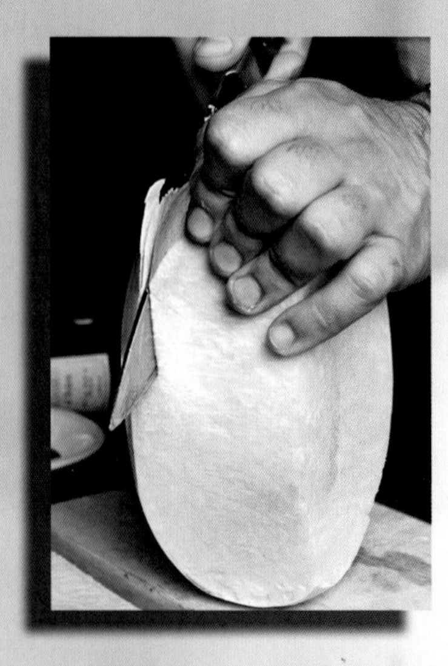

Taking a Spaghetti squash, or any yellow melon. Take a long segment from the skin giving us a melon canvas.

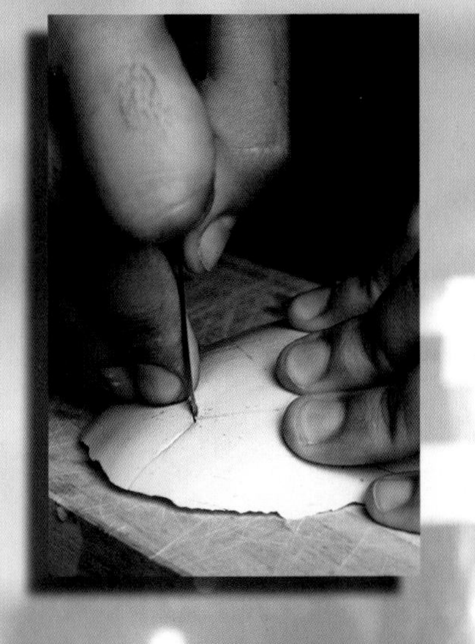

Using a paring knife, lightly carve a stencil on the skin surface in the shape of a fleur-de-lis.

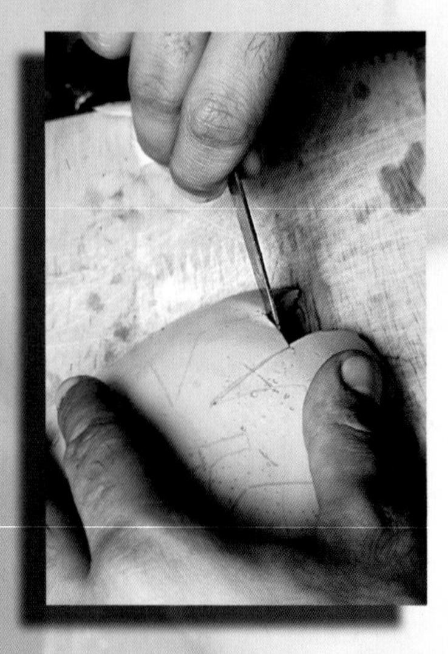

Starting from the top of your stencil, cut out segments of the melon skin to start shaping your garnish from the top center point.

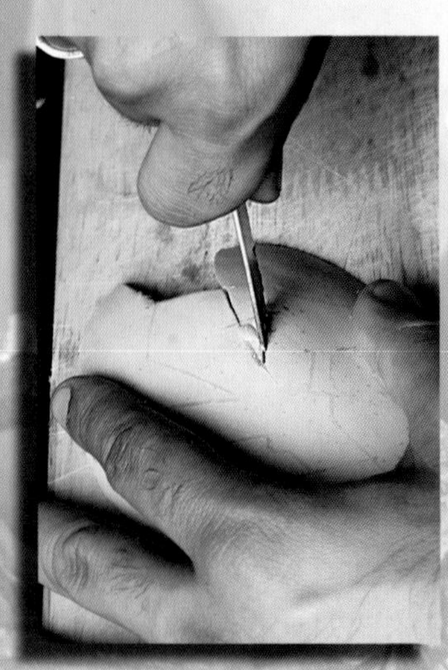

Finish out your fleur-de-lis by making small shaping cuts to the skin so you don't accidentally take a major part out of our garnish.

Make several wedges-like cuts in the melon to remove the skin from the garnish. This will give you the most room to work with the rest of your canvas.

There is a time to work and a time to love – these leave no time for anything else.

__Jacopo Falleni

PASTA BAR

PASTA

by Fabio

I have to introduce to you that thing that I will be miserable living without, Pasta! You can avoid eating every single thing in Italy but you cannot escape from it...you will have pasta for lunch and dinner, no matter what. And, if you are a person that without a medical reason (the only excuse) do not eat pasta for lunch and dinner, you cannot eat at my table. OUT!

There is no way, try to go home, in my house in Florence and after my Mom asks you as soon as you get in the house, let's say for lunch...Are you hungry? You may answer, "no thanks, I ate too much last night and I'm still full," she will smile at you and say, "Okay, don't worry; let me make a little pasta for you." YOU CAN'T SAY NO!

There are two major ways to deal with pasta: a faster, lighter meal, not too pretentious, will use dry pasta, the one without eggs, made from durum wheat flour and water. That will stay best al dente, and please, if you are a person that before you cook the pasta reads the back of the label to check the cooking time rather than stick your hand in the boiling water and taste it, please, take the pasta out two minutes before whatever time they suggest. It's for you, not for me, overcooked pasta will sit in your stomach for hours and will make it swollen. If the pasta with still a little bite or al dente, it will be so much easier to digest.

Next is egg pasta with semolina flour or regular flour but still with fresh eggs inside, that is richer and heavier and goes better for when you have a little bit longer game plan and you can relax after a meal. You cannot have a plate of tagliatelle with meat sauce and Parmesan and afterwards run the NY Marathon. Well, you can but you will not win that is for sure. And, the other factor that I love about fresh eggs, flour and water is all you need besides a fork. People have lost the beauty of the work a little bit in preparing your own meals. But that is okay...that is my job and I have to do it for you. But one day just try and get your hands in the flour and when you taste the result, you will like it better because not only is it good but because you did it.

I think that pasta is one of the first three things that the world has to thank us for, and don't give me crap telling me the Chinese invented it. If they did, shame on them for not sticking with it and making it a big part of their meal. We did and we brought it to the United States!

Second, on the list after pasta is soccer. There, of course, we are masters and the keeper of the World Cup. And then, there is the Renaissance. This is because even if fellows like Michelangelo and Donatello painted the most beautiful cathedral in all of Italy, their art is less edible than a plate of pasta, and there are more people eating pasta with tomato sauce in the world than people going to see a cathedral. That's what I think!

LINGUINE AI FRUTTI DI MARE:
Seafood Linguini
4 servings

Buy 1 lb of a good quality dry pasta Linguine (number 7 is the right size). You will have to cook them for 7-8 minutes in the boiling salted water and then finish it in the sauce with the seafood in order for the pasta to absorb the flavor of the fish.

FOR THE SEAFOOD SAUCE:

8 oz of Heirloom Mixed Color Cherry tomato
8 oz of Fresh Black Mussels
8 oz fresh Manila Clams
1 lb of Fresh Calamari with Tentacles as well
8 oz of Shrimps (size 31/40)
4-5 Claws of Stone Crab - The reason why I choose this crab is because has lots of nice, tasty meat in the Claw. Due to the seasonality of this item it can be substituted with king crab legs, easy to find at the fish (Make-sure-it's-fresh) section of your local market.

½ C Extra Virgin Olive Oil
5 Cloves of garlic
1 C of dry white wine

Bring a pot of water to boil; with a little knife make an x incision on top of the tomato where they use to be attached to the vine, blanch them for about 1½ minutes and drop them in ice water for another 5 minutes. At this point the skin should easily come out, place the tomato in a bowl and set them aside, start the olive oil with the garlic sliced not too thin. Add clams and mussels; let them go in the oil for about 5 minutes covering the top of the pan with a lid. When the shellfish are open, crack the crab claw and add them into the pan. Add the wine and reduce to half on medium fire. Now that the wine is reduced, add the shrimps and the calamari and the tomato.

While you're adding the tomatoes, crush them little bit with your hand so the liquid of the fish will be lightly colored by the tomato, stop the fire and wait for the pasta.

After the pasta is starting to be done (7-8 minutes) add the pasta to the sauce and try to cover the pasta with it. The pasta has to sit in the fish broth in order to get color and flavor. Keep cooking the pasta at medium fire and add also a drizzle of extra virgin olive oil, when the pasta has almost absorbed all the sauce, take the pasta out, plate it and finish with the Fish on top.

JALAPEÑO MARTINI:

1 ½ oz (6 counts) Cachaça
¾ oz (3 counts) Pineapple Puree
2 Tsp of Brown Sugar
2 Lime Wedge (1/3 lime)

2 Red Jalapeno or green
2 Maraschino Cherries
1 Dikon Ruth
15/20 Cloves

PREPARATION
Take your lime, half a jalapeno, depending on how spicy you like, and 2 teaspoons of brown sugar. Muddle them so that the jalapeno can add enough spiciness to the drink. Pour the cachaça followed by the pineapple puree (see glossary). Shake well and serve in a cold, red sugar rimmed Martini Glass.

We are talking of a variation of a refreshing drink of Brasilian tradition "Caipirinha" the color is a very charming green with red veins. The nose is very Caribbean. The taste is sweet with a balanced and unique spice kick at the end.

LA STORIA:
This drink came about due to request of our sous chef, Abel Soriano, who is of Latin heritage. He was tired of margaritas and Corona beer! He wanted something with a Spanish influence that could easily pair with their typical regional food. After several attempts at taco and guacamole martinis ***(bad attempt)*** we hit upon this marvelous and different drink that pairs not only with Latin food but also Italian fish dishes!

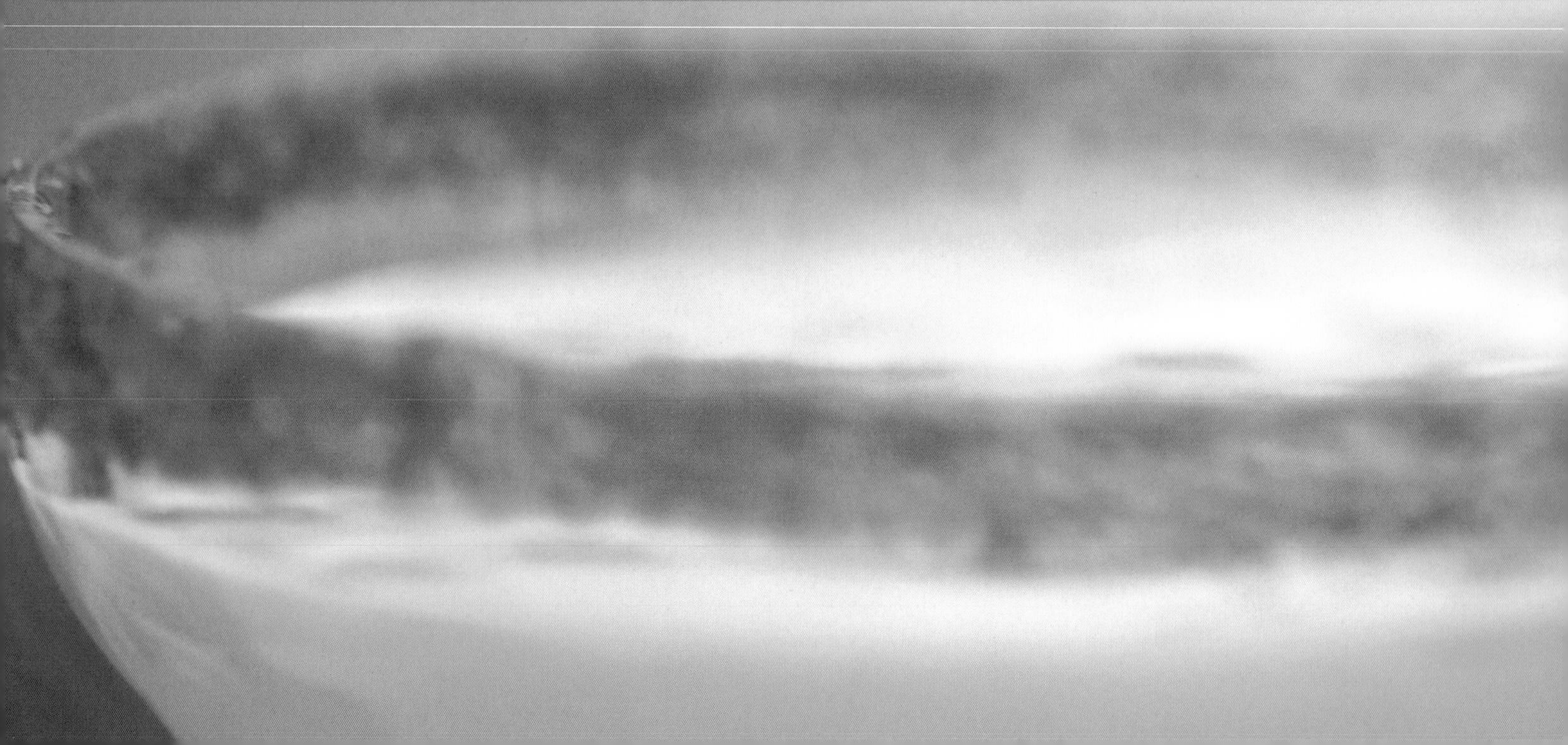

You can teach math, geography & English, but you cannot teach the art of hospitality.

__Jacopo Falleni

Cut a long narrow slice out of a dikon root.

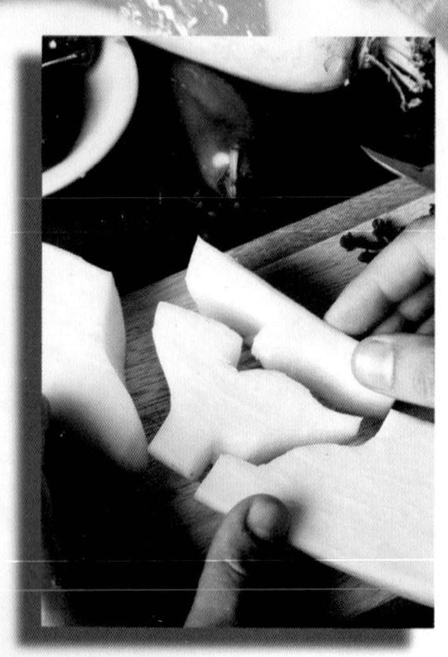

Using a paring knife, shape the slice into two separate "wings."

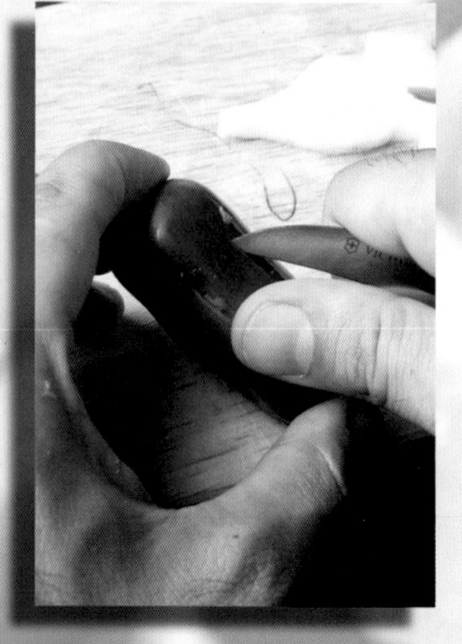

With your bird-beak knife, cut two long vertical holes into a green jalapeno.

Insert each dikon "wing" into the vertical holes in the jalapeno.

Punch several cloves through the dikon wings to add texture and color to the wings.

Finally, poke two small holes using a toothpick at the "top" of the jalapeno. Take two maraschino cherry stems and insert them on the "top" of the jalapeno.

There are two ways of spreading light: to be the candle or the mirror that reflects it.
__Edith Wharton

RAVIOLI CON L'ANATRA E IL MARSALA:

Duck Confit Ravioli with Marsala Reduction
Serves 2

For the Ravioli

4 sheets of fresh pasta
1 C of shredded duck confit
2 potatoes peeled and large diced
¼ C cream
3 Tbsp butter Unsalted
¼ C chopped carrots
¼ C chopped onions
1 Tbsp olive oil
¼ C Parmesan cheese
4 sheets of fresh pasta
1 egg for egg wash

MASHED POTATOES:

In a medium pot add the diced peeled potatoes. Bring to a low boil and cook until fork tender, strain and let sit for 3 min. In a mixing bowl whisk the potatoes with the cream and butter, season to taste with salt and pepper.

FOR THE FILLING:

Sauté the carrots and onions. In a medium bowl mix the vegetables with the shredded duck confit. Add ¼ cup of the mashed potato and season with salt and pepper. Be careful not to over salt. The duck confit is naturally salty. Cut the fresh pasta (see Lobster ravioli recipe) sheets in 2" x 2" squares. Place 1 Tablespoon of the filling in the middle of the square. Brush with egg wash around the edges and pinch the pasta closed, crimp with a fork on a well-floured board. The trick to cooking these raviolis is not to rapid boil the water; you want the water to be at a light boil. Cook the pasta about 4 minutes and toss in the Marsala sauce.

FOR THE MARSALA DEMI:

1Tbsp olive oil
1Tbsp butter
2 large shallots thinly sliced
1 clove of garlic finely diced
1 sprig of thyme fine diced
1 ½ C Marsala wine
2 C veal demi glace - You can buy this in any food store. It is like a gravy mix but much better and tastier. You will fall in love with this and probably you will use this instead of your nasty gravy for your turkey the next Thanksgiving.
3 sprigs of chives chopped for garnish
Salt and pepper

DEMI GLACE:
1 quart of veal stock - You can buy veal stock or beef stock in the food store right next to the chicken stock. Do you see it? Is right there... there you go.
2 oz flour
2 oz butter

Mix butter and flour together in a small sauté pan to make a roux. Cook for 3 min and stir constantly. Set aside, in a small pot bring 2 cups of the veal stock to a boil, add the roux and whisk well to make sure there are no lumps. Add the other two cups of veal stock and reduce by half.

Over medium heat, sauté the garlic, shallots and olive oil. When the shallots are caramelized, add the fresh thyme and season with salt and pepper. Next, deglaze with Marsala and reduce by half. Add the demi glace and reduce. Finish the sauce with 1 Tablespoon of butter and reduce until it's nice and thick. Toss with the raviolis and garnish with fresh chives and shaved Parmesan cheese

DUCK CONFIT RECIPE:

4 duck legs and breast
½ C chopped thyme
4 cloves of garlic chopped
1 orange zest
Salt and pepper to taste
1 qt duck fat or olive oil - enough to fully cover the legs (If you are willing use duck fat. You can find it at some well furnished market, or you can choose to use the same amount of melted butter, little bit heavier than olive oil but more flavorful)

Season the duck legs well with salt, pepper, thyme, garlic and zest, best if let set over night. Rinse off all the seasoning and pat dry. Add the legs and oil or duck fat to medium size pot; be sure to cover the legs completely. Place in a preheated oven at 275 F for 2½ hr or until the meat is shredding off the bone. When the legs are done make sure to let the legs cool down in the duck fat, this will help the duck from losing moisture. When the legs are cooled remove them from the fat and shred the meat with two forks or your fingers.

Sometimes a moment is enough to cause you to forget a lifetime but there are not enough lifetimes to forget a moment.
__Jim Morrison

SANGRALA

½ oz (2 counts) Marsala wine
½ oz (2 counts) Port wine or Vodka
¼ oz (1 count) Pineapple Puree
¼ oz (1 count) Peach Puree
¼ oz (1 count) Banana Liquor
¼ oz (1 count) Peach Liquor
1 oz (4 counts) Santa Margherita Chianti

Fresh raspberries, cherries, lime wedge, orange slice, and lemon slice
2 Oranges

PREPARATION:

Directly in a Goblet glass full of ice pour the Marsala wine and continue to follow the recipe. Make sure you pour the red wine as the last ingredient because it will create a separation effect that looks very good in the glass. You can leave it like that or serve it with a stirrer. An important part of the whole drink is the fresh fruit. Be generous with that to give a yummy look to the all glass!

We are talking of a refreshing drink of Spanish Tradition with a warm red color and a lot of Mediterranean perfumes mixed with the fresh one given by the fruits. The taste is fresh, moderately alcoholic with intense peach aromas accentuated from the one of the wines.

LA STORIA:

Sangria is an alcoholic beverage with a wine base, with spices and fruit, which originated in the Iberian Peninsula. This drink doesn't have just one recipe but multiple variations depending on which Iberian region it has been made. Usually it is made with red wine, but especially in Catalogna, you find some variation of the recipes that are made with Spumante or Sparkling Wine. Originally, this sweet, alcoholic beverage was served between the Spanish farmers who gave it the name referring to its dark, blood red color. Thereby, Spanish for blood is Sangre...Sangria!

Our Sangria has a lot of similarity to the original. Of course, I had to give this Spanish originated drink a touch of the Italianate. Here it is the Marsala showing up in our recipe!
Ladies and Gentleman, please welcome our Sangrala!

Take an orange and slice the top and bottom off.

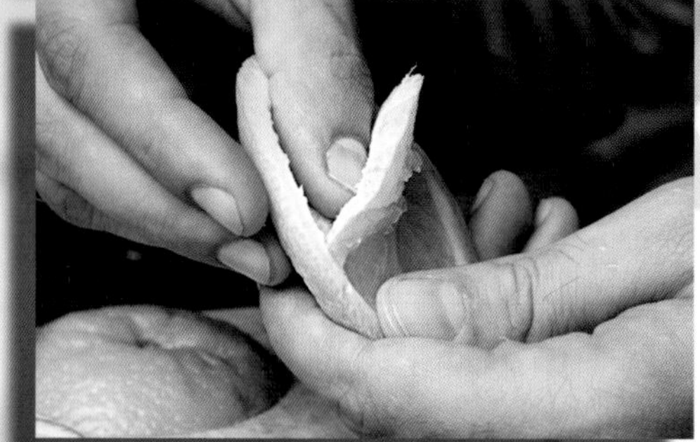

Remove whatever fruit or peeling is left from the inside of the top and bottom.

Using a pointed knife, cut wedge shapes from both the top and the bottom pieces.

Continue removing the wedge shapes to create a star-like shape from both pieces. Remember to make some points of the "star" larger than others (one large, one small, one large, etc.)

Now take a garnish pick and pierce the bottom (the star without the "bellybutton") push the pick through so only a small portion of the end of the pick is protruding.

Finally, with the top star (the one with the bellybutton) pierce into, but not through, the back of the star, giving a layering effect which provides the perfect garnish for our drink.

A person who has not done one half his day's work by ten o'clock, runs a chance of leaving the other half undone.

__ Emily Bronte, English Novelist

RAVIOLI D'ARAGOSTA IN SALSA DI POMODORINI

RAVIOLI D'ARAGOSTA IN SALSA DI POMODORINI:

Lobster Ravioli in a Heirloom Tomato Sauce
4 serving

FOR THE FRESH PASTA:
1.8 Lbs of regular Flour
2 whole Eggs
8 Eggs Yolk
½ Tsp of White Pepper
1 Tbsp of Table salt
2 Tbsp of Water

In a mixer with the hook attachment beat the eggs with the yolk, the water and the salt and pepper. After 5 minutes, when the entire ingredients are mixed together, start to add the flour that you have divided previously in 4 equal parts. Add the first part, then the second, then the third one, for the fourth one, add little by little so you can stop if you see that the dough is becoming too hard. You will realize when it is done because there will not be any trace of the flour around the mixing bowl or in the dough, in case it is still too loose (will stick to your hand), add another 1/2 cup of flour. Then set aside. Dust with flour and wrap in plastic wrap, and place it in the refrigerator for at least 2 hours. If you have a pasta machine, start to roll the pasta, adjusting the thickness each round till you have a really thin layer of pasta. You should be able to almost see the filling inside. If you roll by hand, cut the pasta in smaller pieces and pound them with a meat mallet so will be easy roll them out. Still, you need them thin as possible. Pay attention that the pasta doesn't break.

Once they are rolled out, cut them in rectangles of 2 x 2 inches and store them wrapped in plastic to avoid drying them out. When the filling is ready, place 1 teaspoon of filling in the middle of the square. Brush the outside part of the pasta with egg wash (1 egg plus some water mixed in) and top with another sheet of pasta. Press with the tip of your finger so you will level the thickness of the double sheet. Cook the ravioli for 2 minutes in boiling water and drain them; lay them in a plate coated with the heirloom tomato sauce. Garnish with basil leaf.

FOR THE FILLING:

½ lb of Butter
1 good size Vidalia onion (Vidalia onion is just another name for the Yellow Sweet Onion. You can find them everywhere)
1 Jumbo Carrot
2 Ribs of Celery
4 Cloves of Garlic
1 Whole Lobster (1 ½ Lbs.) American Lobster is the best choice. Not only are you not gonna poke your finger with all the spears of a works-as-well spiny lobster, but you will also get to eat the meat in the claw that our spiny Lobster doesn't have.

1 Bunch of Basil
1 Tbsp of Kosher Salt
1 Tsp of White Pepper
1 C of Brandy

Peel the onion and cut roughly, peel the carrots and cut in chunk, also the celery making sure that you wash. Place the vegetables in a food processor and with the pulse button start to chop them till you have pieces big like a coffee bean. Melt the butter and let the vegetables go inside with the pepper and the whole garlic cloves, cut in half. Add the salt as soon the vegetables start to release part of the water. In the meantime bring water to boil in a pot big enough to contain the whole lobster. Place the lobster in the boiling water for 5 minutes and take that out and place it in an ice bath. Take the lobster out and with a chef knife, section the lobster in half, take the tail meat out; break the claw and take the claw meat out. Now place the rest of the shell in 1 quart of water with little salt and let them simmer so you will have lobster water for the sauce later on.

When you see that the vegetable are nice and caramelized add the lobster tail and claw meat cut in ½ inch squares, let go for 2 minutes. Add the brandy and flambé (light the brandy with a lighter). This will release the alcohol. Once all the brandy is reduced, set the filling aside and let cool down. Once cold, add the basil chiffonade (thinly sliced).

FOR THE POMODORO SAUCE:

1 Lb of Cherry Heirloom Tomato (A true heirloom is a cultivar that has been nurtured, selected, and handed down from one family member to another for many generations, without b***s*** like pesticides, hormones, antibiotics or other stuff that doesn't belong to the diet of anybody.

4 Cloves of Garlic
2 Tbsp of Extra Virgin Olive oil
Kosher Salt
Crushed Black Pepper

Bring a pot of water to boil. With a little knife make an x incision on top of the tomato where they use to be attached to the vine. Blanch them for about 1 ½ minutes and then drop them in ice water for another 5 minutes. At this point the skin should easily come off. Place the tomato in a bowl and set them aside. Start the olive oil with the garlic sliced not too thin; add the tomato and the salt and pepper. Let the tomato go for 10-12 minutes until they release part of the water and become little bit wilted and softer. This sauce will have to go on top of the pasta once on the plate.

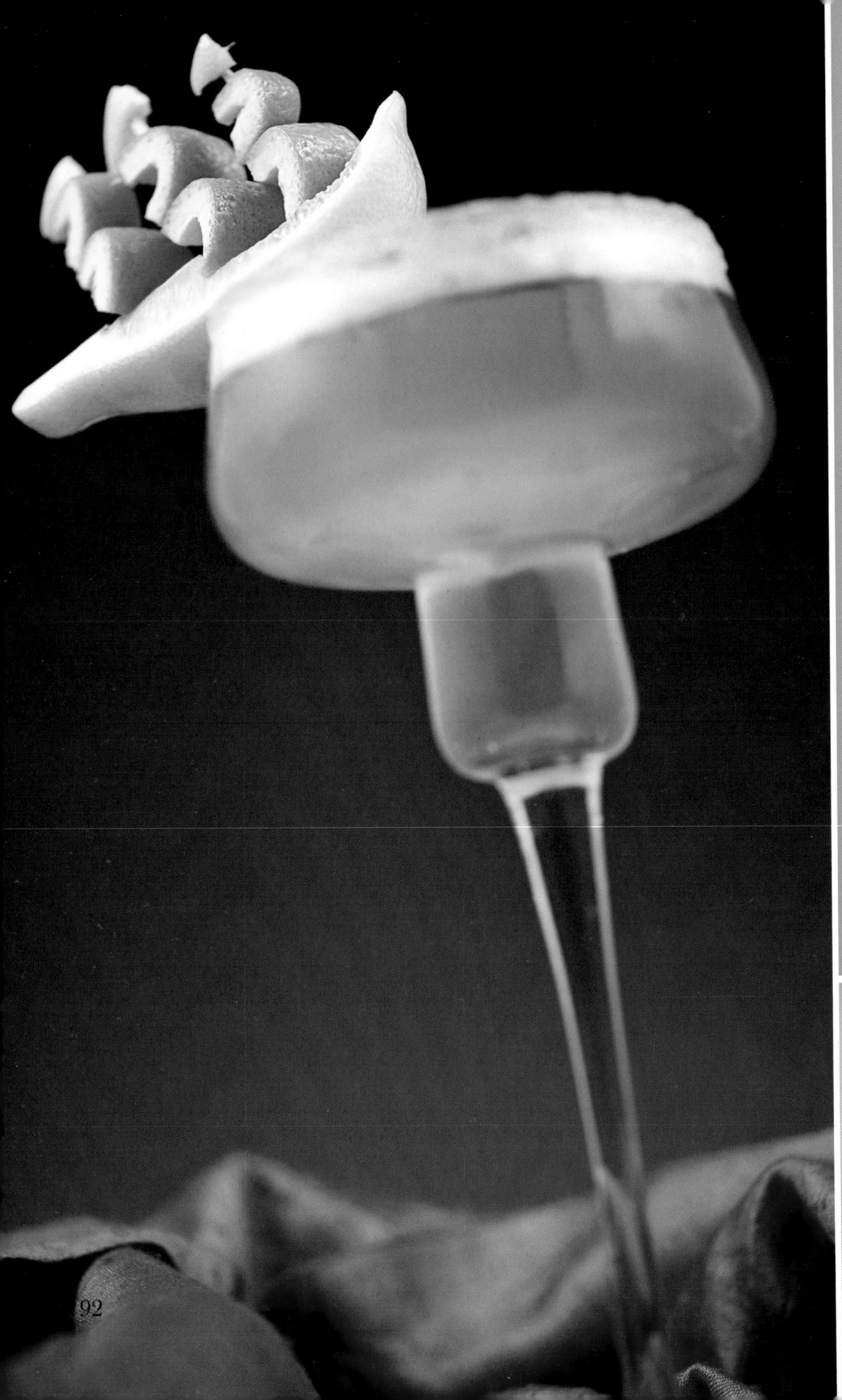

BASIL LEMON DROP

1 ½ oz (6 counts) Citrus Vodka
1 oz (4 counts) Cointreau
½ oz (2 counts) Sweet and Sour
1 squeeze of lemon
4 Basil leaves

1 Orange
1 Lemon

PREPARATION: Take the Basil leaves and cut them by hand then place them in the mixing glass with ½ oz of Sweet and Sour (see glossary). Start muddling until the Sweet and Sour goes from yellow to bright green. Then start pouring the ingredients following the recipe. Shake vigorously, and serve in chilled orange-sugar rimmed glass.

The color is opaque with green reflections. From the strong and predominantly citrusy flavors peep out the fresh basil sensation. The taste is medium sweet with herbaceous fragrances and high alcohol content! Are you going to spend the weekend on the Caribbean beaches where it is 48 Celsius in the shade? Follow my advice and bring this recipe with you!

Using a paring knife, cut a large wedge from a lemon.

From the tip, cut down halfway following the shape of the lemon, once halfway, turn your knife, and continue parallel to the "boat" base, making sure to stop just after half way. Then cut straight down from the top of the lemon to remove the flesh (see picture 7 for shape).

Now take an orange, and remove a large piece of skin.

Cut a long, wide funnel-shape from the skin, then slice the "funnel" in half to create a top and bottom "sail." Repeat twice more.

With a simple toothpick, pierce through the ends of the bottom "sail." then the top "sail" creating the "mast." Make sure to leave a small portion of the pick available at the top of the "mast" Repeat twice more.

Using a small slice of lemon peel, cut three small wedges to be placed at the top of each "mast".

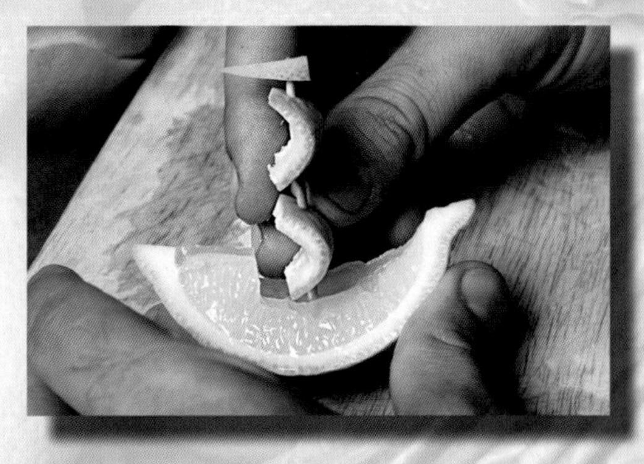

Finally, break two of the three picks at the bottom, so that two of the "masts" are able to pierce into, but not through. Pierce the center "mast" through the entire "boat."

TORTELLI AL GORGONZOLA E NOCI

TORTELLI AL GORGONZOLA, NOCI E FUNGHI:

Gorgonzola Ravioli with Roasted Mushrooms Medley and Walnuts

FOR THE PASTA:

See recipe for the dough of the Lobster ravioli. The only difference is the measure of the square has to be 3 x 3 inches.

FOR THE FILLING:

8 oz Mascarpone Cheese
1 Tsp Hungarian Paprika
Pinch of Salt
1 Russet Potato
10/12 oz Italian Creamy Gorgonzola
6 oz Walnuts
Pinch of crushed Black Pepper
2 C mushroom mix

Peel the potato and boil it in a pot with water till soft, then drain the water and mash with a fork till all the lump are broken down. Add the Mascarpone and the Gorgonzola and season to taste with salt and pepper. Add a little paprika and the walnuts, which have been previously crushed, and half of the mushrooms. Mix. Keep mixing with the back of a fork till the filling looks well mixed. When the filling is ready, place 1 teaspoon of filling in the middle of the square and brush the outside part of the pasta with some egg wash (1 egg plus some water mixed in). Bend one side corner to the other so you now have a perfect triangle; now fold again the opposite angle so you going to have a boat shaped ravioli. Press with the tip of your finger so you will level the thickness of the double sheet. Cook the ravioli for 2 minutes in boiling water and drain them, place them in a serving plate and coated with the mushroom sauce.

FOR THE ROASTED MUSHROOMS:

8 oz Chanterelle mushrooms
8 oz Oyster mushrooms
8 cloves of Garlic
Kosher Salt
1 lb of Butter
1 C of Marsala red Wine
8 oz Hen of Wood mushrooms
3 sprigs of Thyme
1 sprig of Rosemary
Crushed Black Peppercorn
1 C of Chianti red Wine

Clean the dirt from the Mushrooms at the bottom and cut them in 3-4 pieces each. Blanch them in boiling water separating them for type. Each mushroom has a different blanching time and you can feel it from touching the head and the stem. If spongy, they will blanch faster, if firm they will take more time because it won't absorb water as fast as the spongy one. Once done set them in a dry towel. Melt half of the butter with the thyme and the crushed garlic and the rosemary. Let the butter and herbs go for 6-8 minutes on medium fire, add the mushrooms and bring the fire to high. When the edge of the mushrooms are getting a nice brown color is time to add salt and fresh crushed pepper to the mushrooms. Let them cook for 5 minutes, keeping the fire on medium high. Add half of this mixture to the Ravioli filling, and keep the rest aside.

FOR THE GORGONZOLA SAUCE:

2 C of cream
1 C of crumbled bleu cheese
Whole pepper and salt

Bring the cream to boil and put the gorgonzola inside and take out of the fire, stir and add the pepper, fresh grinded, and the salt; coat the ravioli and add some of the crumbled wall nuts.

To the door of the person who laughs, fortune will come.

__Anonymous

ASIAN PERSUASION

1 ¼ oz (5 counts) Vodka
¾ oz (3 counts) Pear Nectar
¾ oz (3 counts) Lychee juice
½ oz (2 counts) Apple Pucker

1 Butternut squash

PREPARATION: This is an easy one. Take your lovely mixing glass; start pouring following the order in the recipe. If you want a stronger taste of lychee, before you start shaking, muddle them!

Shake it well and serve it in a chilled Martini glass.

The color is yellow-green, warm and medium sweet. The drink needs well-ripened lychees so that the smell will be vanilla with sour notes given from the acidity of the Green Apple. Those intense aromas are present not only in the smell but in the taste as well, making it a good after dinner drink.

LA STORIA:

This is in honor of our beloved Mike Takeda, the number guy, the one the works behind the scenes. We all know how stressful his job can be. He can say we take good care of him when he comes late at night downstairs to have a bite and a nice martini!

"Jacopo, can you make something good with lychees?" This is what he usually asks...he loves lychees. Of course, he is Giapponese! Well, he fell in love with this one and it is named for him: The ASIAN PERSUASION!

For this we can use either a round cut (between ½ and 2/3 inch) of either dikon root, or butternut squash.

Using a paring knife, cut a stencil into your "canvas" in the shape of any Asian language character.

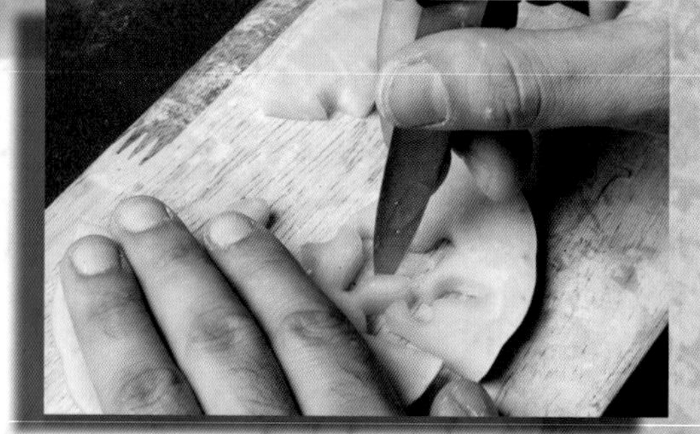

Following your stencil carefully, cut through the canvas remembering to cut out every so often.

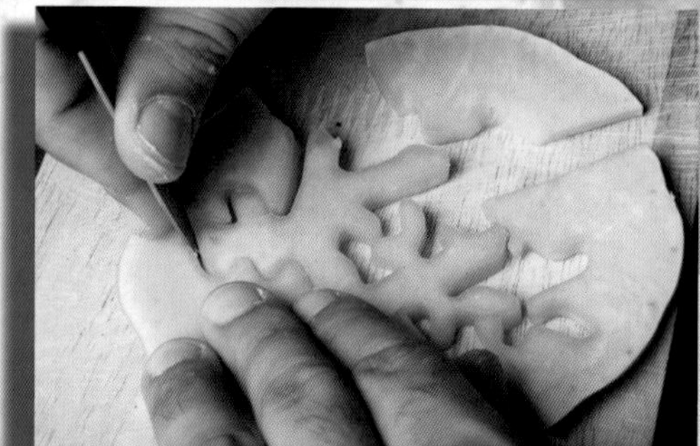

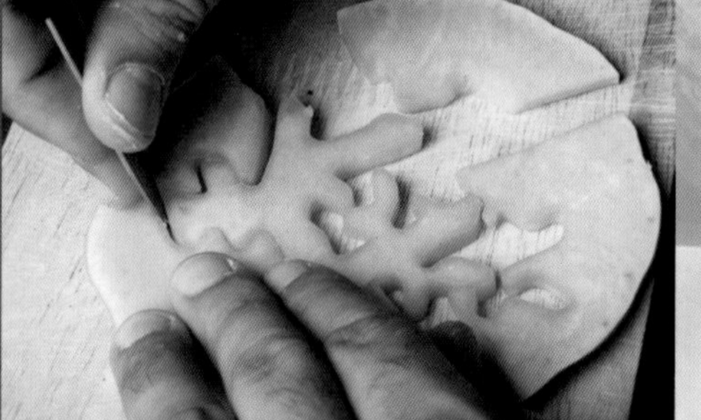

In order to avoid breaking a piece of your garnish off, rotate the sides from which you cut.

Carefully remove any remaining "canvas" from your garnish.

MALFATTI RICOTTA E SPINACI:

Naked Ravioli, Ricotta and Spinach with Brown Butter Sage and Shaved Parmesan
4 servings

FOR THE NAKED RAVIOLI:

3 Lbs of fresh Baby Spinach
2 Lbs of fresh Ricotta cheese
8 oz of Parmesan cheese grated
1 Nutmeg grated
1 Tsp of fresh Ground Black Pepper
2 Eggs
1 Tbsp Kosher Salt
1 Tsp of Baking Soda

Bring to boil a pot with water and add the baking soda. Once it is boiling put all the spinach inside and let cook till the spinach is completely wilted (about 4 minutes). Strain the spinach and with the help of a towel squeeze the water out. Place the spinach on a cutting board and chop them. Not too big...not even completely minced. In a separate bowl, mix all the rest of the ingredient till you have a uniform paste. Don't use any mixer or food processor. You have to use your hand. Once the ricotta mix is ready, add the chopped spinach and keep mixing till you have a uniform clump. It has to be not too white and not too green. It has to look good and you are welcome to add more spinach or ricotta to your taste. In case it is still little too wet, you can dust a hand full of flour, but I wouldn't suggest that. With the help of two spoons shape into quenelle and place it in a tray with non-stick spray on the bottom. Cook in the oven at 500 degrees for about 5 minutes. Let rest for 2-3 minutes and plate with the help of a flat spatula. Be careful or they will fall apart.

FOR THE BROWN BUTTER SAGE SAUCE:

1 Lb of Butter
1 C of Sage leaf
Fresh Ground Pepper
1 C of Water
4 oz of Parmesan

Melt half of the butter in a sauté pan with the sage leaf and the black pepper. When the sage and the butter start to get golden brown, add the pepper and the water little by little. Keep stirring and adding water on low fire till you have a creamy, velvet butter sauce. In case it looks separated or too oily, add warm water; if too runny or too watery, keep on the fire and reduce. Once thickened in the right way, coat the naked ravioli as much as you like.

Top the naked ravioli with shaved Parmesan; use a peeler to get really thin shaving.

Café Firenze
FABIO VIVIANI

Life is the flower to which love is the honey
__Victor Hugo

TRANQUILITY

1 ¼ oz (5 counts) Pear vodka
¾ oz (3 counts) Triple sec
½ oz (2 counts) Pineapple Puree
½ oz (2 counts) Homemade Sweet and Sour
1 squeeze of lemon
Hand full of diced cucumbers
6 Sage leaves
1 Zucchini squash

PREPARATION: Place the diced cucumbers in the mixing glass. Add ½ oz of Sweet and sour and muddle well. Make sure that the cucumber pulls out all the juice and the watery parts. Once you create the base following the recipe, start pouring all the ingredients. Remember that you already used the ½ oz of Sweet and Sour. Don't pour them again, otherwise you drink will be pretty tart!

Shake it and serve it in a nice chilled and green-sugar rimmed Martini glass.

The drink has a beautiful greenish-yellow color and a flowing texture from the floating cucumber seeds. The perfume is very inviting. Between the fresh vegetal tones we can easy recognize the fresh pineapple. The taste is soft, light, refreshing and very balanced. The perfect match for a nice and relaxing spa treatment!

LA STORIA: The way we created the name of this martini is diabolical. During a meeting prior to the opening of the restaurant, my bar staff and I were trying to find recipes, names and categories for all the new drinks. We thought it would be nice and catchy to make a sort of healthy martini line. We created a very original spa martini list where you can find drinks like Tranquility, Ginger Serenity, Relaxitini and Joymartini. It seems funny but the name is the first thing that the customer is attracted to...that's why they are so popular!

Take the zucchini and shave five pieces off (about as wide as your thumb) exposing the outside of our "flower."

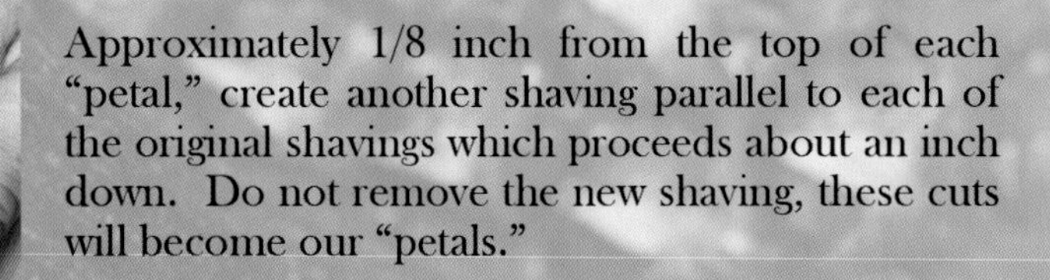

Approximately 1/8 inch from the top of each "petal," create another shaving parallel to each of the original shavings which proceeds about an inch down. Do not remove the new shaving, these cuts will become our "petals."

Remove the rest of the zucchini from the "flower" so we have the canvas to create the inside of our "flower" (this is where it may get a little complicated).

Make a cut from the middle of the inside of each petal, and remove the flesh from the petal to your new cut.

Using the same two-cut system from steps 1 and 2, make another cut, approximately an eighth of an inch (towards the middle) from the last set of cuts which is parallel to each of the 5 new cuts (this creates 5 new "half petals").

Follow steps 4 and 5 once more, then scar the middle of the "flower" with your knife a few times to create the stamen.

Make a small incision at the base of our "flower" to create the resting place for our garnish.

Nothing gives one person so much advantage over another as to remain always cool and unruffled under all circumstances.

__Thomas Jefferson

PESCE - FISH

FISH

by Fabio

In Italy, fish is about quality. More and more often it happens that you go to a fish restaurant in Italy close to the pier in the town where you are spending your holiday and on the menu you will find just a couple of selections instead of 10 or 15 different selections of fish that you will be able to find in most high-end restaurants in America.

In Italy there is no fish available that was caught in the ocean yesterday...there are no frozen fish selections and no vacuum-sealed process that can prolong the freshness.

You can eat fish that has been sitting in the refrigerator for three days, absolutely yes. But for the best quality, I get fish for my restaurant delivered every day and when the fish is not today's catch, we don't have fish on the restaurant's menu because if the best selection is not possible to get we don't take chances to present an average product.

In Italy we say, "if you have a good piece of fish, leave it alone." The less you touch it the better it will taste meaning that a good piece of fresh fish needs nothing but fire to be cooked, some salt, olive oil and maybe some lemon. Of course, international cuisine teaches us to play with food and pair it with important combinations of flavors. But if you go there, in my country, you will have your fish, whole, with bones, head on and probably still moving and you have to kill it, then you will compare 'my-way-fish' with what you are used to from today's market, in some of the restaurant here in America and then you let me know.
You need to tell your sales person at the market that the fish smell is little bit strong, that you don't like the color that the flesh has, that you think that this fish that you are about to buy at the market is not really fresh, and you will see that if a large amount of people will do this on a regular basis, the markets where you go now, and the restaurants where you've been eating and the fish was not so great, will start to carry fewer products but more quality.

Give a man a fish and you will feed him for a day – teach him to fish and you will feed him all his life.

__Unknown

BRANZINO CON I POMODORINI E VERDURE:
Striped Sea Bass with Cherry Tomato and Vegetables
4 servings

FOR THE FISH AND VEGETABLES:

4 Striped Sea Bass filet 8/10 oz each (for this recipe you will need in absence of Snapper, another fish where the whole filet doesn't exceed 10 oz. You want to avoid big fish such as tuna, mahi, escolar or sword fish. Look for smaller fish, like the not-too-refined-tilapia, or some smaller trout, or any other kind of fish that when whole is not bigger than 2 lbs. This is the whole beauty of this plate: to serve the whole filet as single portion.

Fresh Ground Pepper
Fleur de Sel
8 oz of Heirloom Cherry Tomato
2 Green Zucchini
20 Asparagus
¾ Baby Carrots
1 C of good Extra Virgin Olive Oil

Salt and pepper the fish on both sides. Start a sauté pan on high fire with 2 Tbsp of oil. When the oil is smoking hot, place the sea bass skin down first. Press the flesh with a spatula or the fish will bend. After 3-4 minutes the skin will be nice, brown and crispy. Turn the fish on the other side; cook for 2 more minutes and set aside. When the tomato and vegetables are ready, finish the fish in the oven at 500 degrees for 2 minutes.

Bring a pot of water to boil. With a little knife make an x incision on top of the tomato where they used to be attached to the vine. Blanch them for about 1½ minutes and drop them in ice water for another 5 minutes. At this point the skin should easily come off. Place the tomato in a bowl and set them aside.

Cut the zucchini in half and slice them ¼ inches. Set them aside, cut the asparagus and keep just the top 2 inches, cut the baby carrots in quarters length wise and set them aside.

Using the boiling water from the tomato, blanch all the rest of the vegetables for 2-3 minutes each.

When done, season the veggie with fresh ground pepper and kosher salt, let them go all at once in a really hot sauté pan with very little oil so they will caramelize fast.
Display the vegetables and the cherry tomato in the bottom of the plate and top with the fish right out from the oven.

Finish with some tomato water. Add some basil leaf.

FOR THE TOMATO AND BASIL WATER:

6 Ripe Beef Steak Tomato
4 Shallots
4 Cloves of Garlic
Kosher Salt
2 Meyer Lemon
1 Sprig of Thyme
1lb of Basil

Chop the shallots and the garlic and let them go with thyme in a sauté pan with 2/3 spoon of extra virgin olive oil. Cut the tomato beefsteak in quarters and let them cook, mixing them with the shallots for at least 30 minutes on low. Add 2 tbsp of salt and the juice of the 2 lemons. Add one gallon of water and bring to boil over medium high heat. When it starts to boil reduce the heat to medium low. Reduce the liquid to half, mixing once in a while. When the broth is reduced, add the basil leaf and let infuse the broth for 10 minutes. Using a china cup, strain the liquid and then filter the liquid again using cheesecloth. Pour some broth over the cherry tomato and vegetables in the plate. Place the fish right out of the oven on top.

Finish with fleur de sel and fresh ground pepper.

One must ask children
and birds how cherries and strawberries taste. __Johann Wolfgang von Goethe

BLOODY MARIO
¾ oz (or 3 counts) Tomato Vodka
1 ½ oz (or 6 counts) Tomato Puree
¾ oz (or 3 counts) Italian Style Bloody Mary mix

1 Watermelon

PREPARATION:

Who has never had, after a rough night at the Club, a nice and chilled Bloody Mary? Is it the best drink ever for a hangover? Isn't it? This is inspired from the original version with, of course, an Italian flair of ingredients.

The recipe is prepared directly in the long drink glass with ice. Take your Italian mix, (see glossary) pour 3/4 oz over ice, add the ¾ oz or of vodka, and finish it with the fresh tomato juice. Mix it with the mixing spoon until the ingredients are very well blended.

Very important for the way your drink turns out is the right proportion of the sauce, the spices and the use of a very well done tomato juice. That is number one ingredient.

The strong power of the vodka and the acidity of the lemon mellow the strong taste of the tomato that is highlighted from the warmness of the spices and the exotic sauces.

This is a complex drink, very different. Good as pre-dinner drink as well as paired to a savory plate.

LA STORIA:

The idea to mix vodka with tomato Juice began in 1920 when Ferdinando Petriot, Barman of Harry's Bar of Paris opened.

This recipe was having an incredible success especially with the American public that hung out at his bar. Within time, the recipe was enriched with all the other spices and the deep red color was the reason why we know this recipe as bloody Mary, which refers to Mary, Queen of Scots.

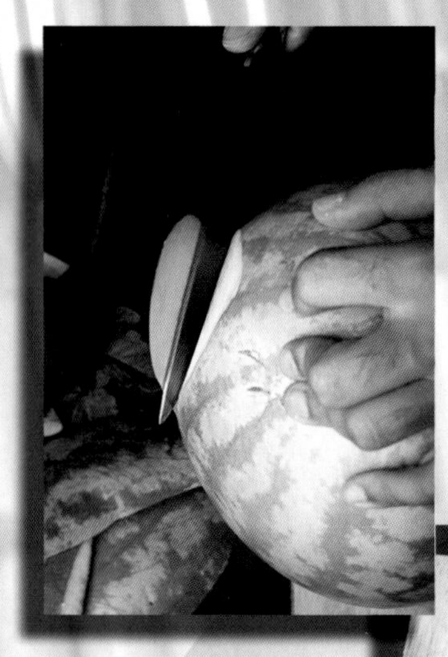

Cut off a vertical segment of the watermelon rind, giving us a nice sized canvas.

Always start with your simple lines first. Cut from the top of the "breast" with a nice curved line about the length of your pinky finger. Then branch out creating a "perch" for our garnish to rest on. Make a small curve under your perch, then a diagonal line down with another small curve to create the front of the "tail."

Cut back up with a large curve, stopping opposite the perch, to finish the tail. One small wedge-cut (curved upwards), one large wedge-cut (also curved upwards) and a final small wedge-cut (you guessed it! Curved upwards) creates the tips of our bird's wings. With a large almost semi-circular cut we create the back of the "bird" and with a small curve at the end we shape the back of our "bird's" head.

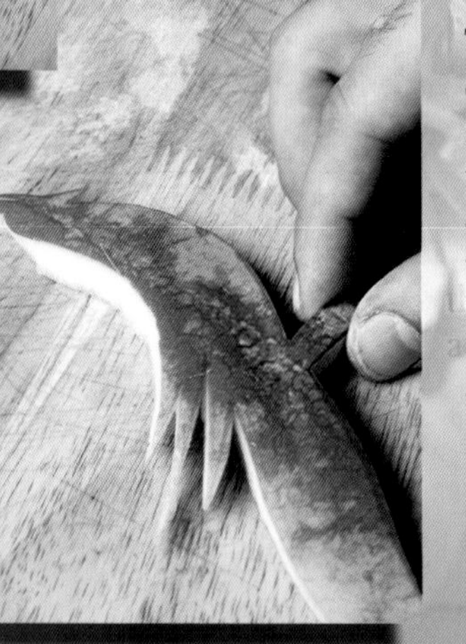

Three consecutive pointed wedges (all in the same directions) create the "bird's head feathers." A simple wedge at the front creates the "bird's beak." Lastly a small cut upwards where the "perch" meets the "tail" will provide a nice resting place for our garnish.

ARAGOSTA AL FORNO CON ASPARAGI BIANCHI E VERDI E SALSA BERNAISE AL TARTUFO

ARAGOSTA AL FORNO CON ASPARAGI BIANCHI E VERDI E SALSA BERNAISE AL TARTUFO

Roasted Lobster with White and Green Asparagus and Truffle Bernaise
4 serving

FOR THE LOBSTER AND THE ASPARAGUS

4 Each Pacific Lobster no bigger than 1 lb
16 White Asparagus big size
16 Green Asparagus big size
Fresh Black Pepper ground
Fleur de Sel
3 Carrots
2 Onions
2 Ribs of Celery
1 Tbsp of Black Peppercorn
2 Sprigs of Thyme
1 Stick of Butter

Bring a large pot of water to boil. Chop coarsely the carrots, onion, and celery, put them in the water, add the peppercorn, and the sprig of thyme. Let boil for at least 1 1/2 hours so that the vegetables and the Herbs release the flavor in the water. This bouillon is good also for other kinds of poached fish. Bring the heat to medium and place the lobster in the pot. Let simmer for at least 5-6 minutes, or till the shell has turned dark red. Take the lobster out and discard the bouillon. Take the tail apart and cut open in half, lengthwise. Take the meat out trying not to break it. Crack the claw using a meat mallet or the back of a knife. Pull the claw meat out, paying attention so you don't break it. Now set the meat aside in an oven pan. Crush some pepper on it, some fleur de sel and a little chunk of butter here and there. In the meantime, peel both types of asparagus with a potato peeler. The goal here is to take off the very external layer of skin so they will be more tender and tasty. Once all are peeled, blanch them in a pot with boiling water for 3-4 minutes and set them aside.

FOR THE TRUFFLE BERNAISE SAUCE

5 Egg Yolks
2 Shallots
1 Lb of Butter
2 Tbsp of Truffle Olive Oil
1 Medium size Truffle in jar (1.5-2 oz) or fresh if available
1 Tsp of Kosher Salt
1 C of White Wine

Peel the shallots and slice them really thin. Let them go with ½ stick of butter till golden brown. Add the wine and keep reducing the sauce till you have a creamy smooth consistency. Keep the foam separated. Strain the shallot liquid and set aside. Put a little pot of water on medium fire and place the egg yolks in a bowl. Place the bowl on the pot with the simmering water in it and start to whisk the yolks. They will start to foam and triple in volume. Also the color will change from deep orange to light Yellow. When the yolks are ready, start to add the melted butter little by little, whisking to incorporate evenly. Half way through the incorporation of the butter, add little by little the juice from the reduction of the shallots. Once all is incorporated, finish adding the butter and keep whisking till smooth and no trace of liquid fat is still visible. Add the truffle oil and the truffle, previously minced with a good knife or a mini-food processor, (like coffee grinder). Place the lobster in the oven at 450 degrees for 3-4 minutes and reheat the asparagus. Season the asparagus and place them in the bottom of the plate with the lobster on top, serving to each guest the whole tail and the 2 claws. Coat the top of the lobster with the sauce. Drizzle remaining on and around the plate.

Love and food are taken seriously by Italians.
__Anonymous

NEGRONI
1 oz (4 counts) Gin
1 oz (4 counts) Vermouth Rosso
1 oz (4 counts) Bitter Campari

1 Orange

PREPARATION: The Negroni is prepared in the old fashion glass filled with ice. Make sure, before you start pouring, there is no water from melted ice in the glass. Now we start! Gin goes in first then Vermouth Rosso and finally Campari. Mix quickly with a cocktail spoon and complete it with the orange slice as a decoration!

The target color for this drink is ruby red. The nose is intense with sweet and bitter, astringent spices mixed with juniper berry, orange, and vanilla flavors. All these sensations are found in the taste along with a warm, dry and big body that leaves a pleasant bitter sensation! This is definitely the king of the Aperitif drinks!

LA STORIA:

The Negroni is one of the most requested drink during Italian "Aperitivo". Aperitivo is a religious moment for us...I miss it a lot. It is the social time that every Italian spends at the bar drinking and eating while waiting to go to the restaurant. This is the Italian version of the American Happy Hour! The only difference, besides being all dressed up, is that food is served and the drink is more expensive.

The drink owes its name to an aristocrat who, in the 1920s, hung out at Il Café Casoni (today's Bar Giacosa). Count Camillo Negroni would order an Americano drink made with red Vermouth and Bitter Campari, which was very trendy at the time! One night, he asked the Bartender, Fosco Scarselli, to add some gin to his drink and of course he liked it! Many regulars started to order Mr. Negroni's Americano version! If you are able to read Italian and you wish to know the amazing story behind the number one Italian cocktail, my mentor, Luca Picchi wrote an entire book, *Sulle Tracce Del Conte*, on the story of these Florentine wonders!

Very Simple! Very Beautiful! Cut an orange in half, then cut a quarter inch orange wheel off of the half.

Using a paring knife, cut along the inside of the orange skin leaving just a little room between the fruit and the knife, leaving about one inch of the skin attached.

Pull the skin of the orange off, giving you a nice sized "twist" which is still attached to the orange wheel.

Tie the twist into a loose knot and drop the fruit into the drink, leaving the "twist knot" sitting against the rim of the glass.

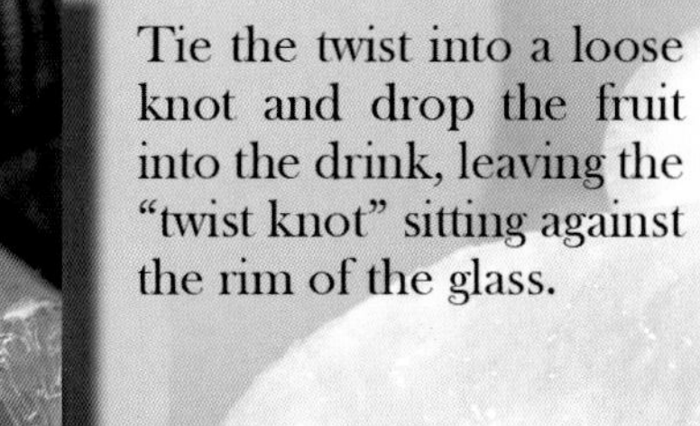

SOGLIOLA SALTIMBOCCA E RIDUZIONE DI SYRAH:

Dover Sole Saltimbocca with Syrah reduction
4 servings

4 Petrale or Dover Sole filet (12-14 oz each, cleaned and skinless - ask your Fish Guy)
1 Bunch of Basil
3 Zucchini Yellow or Green
Fresh Ground Black Pepper
½ C of Olive Oil

One whole side of Sole is made up with 2 single smaller filets. Separate them, cutting them length-wise with a knife. Place on top of them a slice of plastic wrap and pound them very little, just to even the level of the flesh, but make sure that you don't smash any of the meat. Grind some pepper on the filet and add a little salt. Set them in the refrigerator. Now you have 8 single filet-strips.

Slice the zucchini very thin with a knife or mandolin. Add some seasoning and drizzle with some extra virgin olive oil. Place them in the oven in an oven pan at 450 degrees, and let them get golden brown. You will have to move them every 5 minutes or they will burn on the side. Pay attention that you don't break them. When they are done let them cool down and remove them from the oven pan.

Remove the plastic from the fish and place some of the zucchini all over the length of the filet with some basil leaf and roll the filets. When rolled, secure them with a toothpick. When all 8 of them are completed, place them again in the refrigerator while waiting for the sauce.

FOR THE SYRAH REDUCTION:
3 C of Syrah
½ lb of Butter
4 Shallots
1 Sprig of Thyme
Fresh ground Pepper
Kosher Salt

Peel the shallots and slice them really thin. Let them go with one spoon of butter and the thyme sprig and some salt and pepper. When the shallots are golden brown, deglaze with the wine and let the sauce reduce to half. At this point add the butter and turn the heat on medium low, reducing till the sauce reaches a smooth creamy consistency; has to be able to coat the back of a spoon, now the sauce is ready.

In order to cook the sole filet, place a cast iron or non-stick pan on the fire with very little oil and a single spoon of butter, when the oil is really hot, place the sole filet, four at time, standing on the rolled edge. When crisp and brown, turn them on the other side, and when done remove them from the pan. Set them in a cooling rack ready to go in the oven, cook the rest of the sole and when done, place all 8 of them in the oven that has been preheated at 475 degrees for 3-4 minutes max.

Remove the sole rolls from the oven and plate them, drizzle with the wine sauce on top and around the plate.

He can who thinks he can, and he can't who thinks he can't.
– Pablo Picasso

LA STORIA:
The blackberry has always fascinated me. In my language we call it Mora. And when I was little, my grandmother used to tell me stories about how long ago, all over Europe, people would plant blackberry bushes over the graves of their loved ones who had passed away. It was said that the thorns on the bushes would keep evil spirits from disturbing their beloved. Others said that the berries themselves would scare the ghosts away. All I know is that I was afraid of Blackberries for years and no one could ever figure out why! But now, obviously, I love them. And they are incredibly good for you too; loaded with antioxidants!

BLACKBERRY THYME CAIPRINHA

1 ½ oz (6 counts) Chacaça or blackberry vodka
¾ oz (3 counts) simple syrup
3 lime wedges (half-lime)
1 thyme sprig
3 blackberries

1 Honeydew Melon

PREPARATION:

Take three lime wedges and place them in a rock glass with ¾ oz simple syrup (see glossary). Add the Blackberries and the thyme. Muddle to bring the aroma out of your spices. You should now have a pulp with a purplish color in your glass - taste it for balance. Need more sugar or acid? Continue by adding the 1 ½ oz of Cachaça. Now fill your glass with ice, shake it hard and serve it in a nice rock glass. The good part of this drink is the smashed fruit floating so make sure you do not strain it!

This is a refreshing drink inspired from a famous one of Brazilian tradition: "the Caipirinha."

The color is purple, with dark veins; the perfume is strongly dominated by the Caribbean essence of lime and balanced from the delicate thyme fragrance. The drink is thick and pulpy, very tasty and well-balanced.

Take a Honeydew melon and slice a large piece of the skin from the melon.

Cut and remove the skin on the base of the skyline.

Now take a stencil of the most beautiful skyline in the world (of course I'm talking about Firenze) and place on top of the melon. Using a paring knife cut the guidelines into the skin, and move the stencil. Start by cutting the top right portion of the skyline away, removing the excess skin at the top of the first tower.

Now from the left side of the base, cut and remove the skin from the top of the skyline remembering to remove the excess at the top of the second tower. (You've come so far, don't forget to remove the excess at this point so we don't lose the entire garnish.)

Finally cut and carefully remove the piece of melon skin in between the two towers in the middle, finishing our garnish.

IPPOGLOSSO CON POLENTA E ASPARAGI E PEPERONI AL FORNO

IPPOGLOSSO CON POLENTA E ASPARAGI E PEPERONI AL FORNO:

Halibut with Polenta, Asparagus and roasted Bell Pepper
4 servings

FOR THE VEGETABLES:

16 Green Asparagus - size big
1 Bell Pepper Yellow
Fresh Ground Pepper
1 bunch of Basil
1 Bell Pepper Red
Kosher Salt
½ C of Olive Oil

Peel the asparagus with a potato peeler, the goal here is the take off the very external layer of skin so they will be more tender and tasty; once are all peeled blanch them in a pot with boiling water for 3/4 minutes and set them aside.

Grill the bell pepper or place them in the oven at 475 degrees till the skin is burned and bubbling. Take them out and wrap them in plastic wrap and let them to cool to room temperature. Once cold, peel the skin off and cut them with a knife, after discarding the seeds, really thin. Season with salt and black pepper, a little bit of olive oil and some basil leaf.

Roast the asparagus in extra virgin olive oil in a sauté pan till they are brown and crisp. Season with salt and pepper.

FOR THE POLENTA:

1 C of Polenta or Grits
1 Tbsp of Salt
1 C of Heavy Cream
1 C of Water (or 2 cups of Water if you don't want to use any Heavy Cream)
1 Tbsp of Chopped Rosemary
3 Cloves of Garlic
½ Lb of Butter
1 Tsp of Fresh Ground Pepper

Let the butter go with the rosemary and the garlic sliced really thin, add the salt and pepper. Add the cream and the water. Bring to boil, add the polenta or grits and lower the fire to medium-low till the consistency of the polenta is thick but still creamy, like a spread. Taste for salt or pepper. At this point, replace the fish in the oven at 475 degrees for 4-5 minutes. Put a spread of polenta on the bottom of the plate, the fish on top, the asparagus on the side and a little bit of peppers on the top of the fish, drizzle with little olive oil.

FOR THE HALIBUT:

4 pieces of Halibut 8 oz each
Kosher Salt
Fresh ground Pepper
½ C of Oil

Season the halibut with the salt and fresh ground pepper. Drizzle the fish with the oil. Turn the fire on medium high and when the grill is really hot, place one piece of fish at a time on the grill. Sear the fish on each side; they have to look nicely brown and crispy. Then place them in a cooling rack, waiting for the vegetables to be done.

Celebrated for its sophisticated, food-friendly taste, Santa Margherita Pinot Grigio is a great favorite at Cafe Firenze.

BELL PEPPER SEDUCTION

1 ½ oz (6 counts) Vanilla Vodka
½ oz (2 counts) Grapefruit Juice
½ oz (2 counts) Pineapple Puree
½ oz (2 counts) Simple Syrup
Small handful of diced red Bell Pepper
1 Squeeze of Lemon

1 Watermelon

PREPARATION:
In the mixing glass place a handful of fine diced red bell pepper followed by ½ oz of simple syrup (see glossary). Muddle them for about ten second until the syrup becomes red and extracts all the flavors from the pepper. Add all the other ingredients following the recipe: vanilla vodka, grapefruit juice, pineapple puree (see glossary) and a squeeze of lemon. Fill the shaker with ice. Shake it hard and pour it in a chilled martini glass rimmed with red sugar.

This is an unusual drink but most of all an unusual product to work with in a bar! That's why we love it! The drink has a very attractive orangey-pink color. The nose makes you think of the last farmer's market that you visited! The mouth is an unforgettable and unique flavor – it has a little of every sense: the sweet of the vodka and the pineapple, the bite of the grapefruit juice, the acid of the lemon and the beautiful earthy aftertaste of the bell pepper! It is so good that after I came up with this recipe Fabio had to go to AA!

LA STORIA:
There is not always a perfect story for every drink. Sometimes it is just like writing a book. You are not always in the mood. You just get inspiration, and inspiration is when the right word and right thoughts come from your mind – that's pretty much what happens behind the bar. I look around and see the bottle that is looking at me, and then I step into the kitchen and find the ingredient that I have never used and start working. And, here we go! The bell pepper martini is on your table!

If you are going to walk on thin ice,
you might as well dance.
__ Anonymous

Using a watermelon skin canvas and a paring knife, carefully outline the delicate pose of the woman shown in the final picture. Cut and carefully remove the canvas from the chest to the end of the outstretched leg.

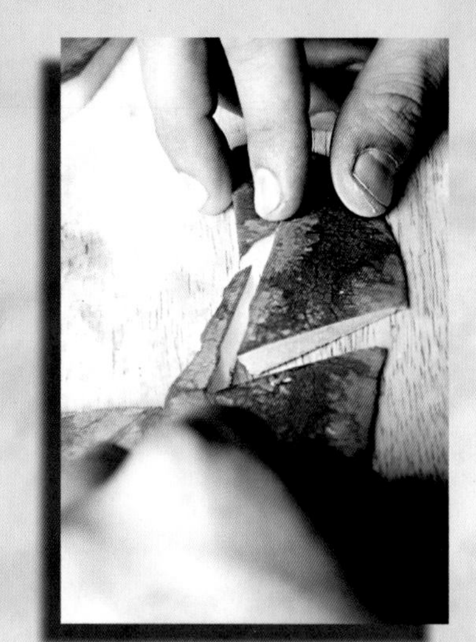

Then cut and remove the canvas around the rest of the outstretched leg.

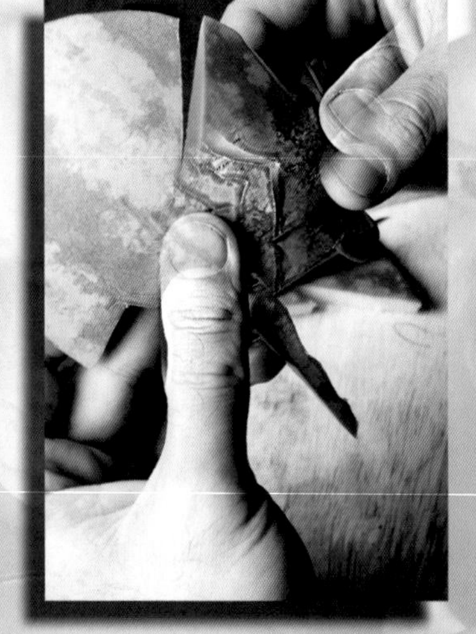

Next, we cut around the end of the bent leg and remove at the tip of the foot.

Now, focus on the other side of the woman's body, carefully cutting and removing the canvas at the tip of the woman's hand.

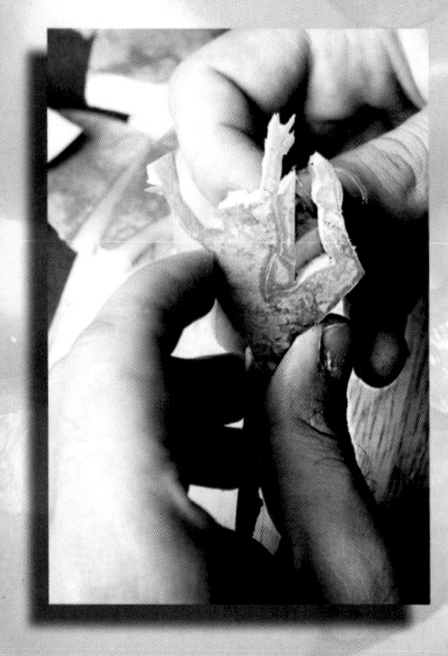

Last, carefully cut around the hand, down the arm, a small semi-circle for the "face," up the outstretched arm, carefully cut around the hand making small wedges for the fingers Then very carefully cut the inside canvas around the outstretched hand and bent leg. Cut a small wedge in between the legs giving a perfect resting place for our garnish. It looks very good!

RANA PESCATRICE RIPIENA CON SALSA DI MELAGRANE:

Rolled Monk Fish with Pomegranate Sauce
2 servings

FOR THE FISH:

8 oz monkfish cleaned (I'm sorry but this recipe has to be done with Monkfish, this particular filet has the perfect round shape to be sectioned and wrapped around anything you may want to put inside.)
5 slices of Prosciutto Parma
2 big asparagus spears
2 Tbsp of Olive Oil
Salt
Pepper

Place the five slices of prosciutto side-by-side, overlapping each other ¼ in. Set aside. For the monkfish, make a slice in the middle from top to bottom. Be sure not to cut all the way through the fish. Now season the fish front and back with salt and pepper. Take the asparagus, after peeling them, and blanch them in boiling water. Let the asparagus go in a sauté pan with pepper and salt for couple of minutes till it is starting to brown, for 4 minutes and place it in middle of the fish. Then place the fish on top of the prosciutto slices. Now you roll the prosciutto over the fish like you would with a sushi roll. Pre-heat a medium non-stick sauté pan with the 2 Tbsp of olive oil in the pan. Place the fish in the pan and turn the heat down to a medium flame. Sauté the fish on all sides until the Prosciutto is golden brown all the way around.

Place in an oven about 4–5 minutes or until the fish is cooked. Let the fish rest about 3 minutes before slicing. Now cut into ½ inch medallions and drizzle with the pomegranate reduction.

FOR THE POMEGRANATE SAUCE:

2 C of pomegranate juice
1 Tsp chopped thyme
2 Tbsp balsamic reduction
1 Tsp butter
Salt and pepper

Place all the ingredients into a medium sauté pan. Over medium heat reduce the sauce until it coats the back of your spoon.

POMEGRANATE MARGARITA

1 ½ oz (6 counts) Tequila Silver
1oz (4 counts) Orange liqueur or triple sec
½ oz (2 counts) Fresh pomegranate juice
½ oz (2 counts) Ginger syrup
2 lime wedges
1 Fresh ginger root

1 Lime
1 Pomegranate

PREPARATION:
In a mixing glass place a pinch of fresh ginger root. Add the ginger syrup (see glossary) and muddle it softly...the ginger has a very strong flavor and you don't want to overdo it! Following the recipe, add the tequila, the triple sec, the fresh pomegranate, and the juice of two limes.

Fill the shaker with ice. Shake it until cold, and then strain into a chilled apple sugar rimmed long drink glass.

Nothing can look so refreshing...a nice chilled glass with a bright green rim and a dark pink drink. The essence is dominated from the spicy acidic characteristics of the ginger. The mouth is a mixture of opposite sensations of spice (ginger) and Sweetness (pomegranate), with the nice kick of the base spirits!

LA STORIA:

I have always associated pomegranates with romance. I'm sure it's because of their deep reddish purple color and they are so amazing, who wouldn't love them? I guess it's that or maybe just that Italians associate everything with romance! They are a luscious fruit to use and believe me, with that little extra zest of ginger, this drink redefines the term "Happy Hour!"

Using the "button" (the physical piece of the lime which attaches to the branch) as a guideline, cut down into the lime about 2/3 of the way.

Repeat using the other side of the "button" as a guideline for your second cut.

Cut small triangle wedges into the "rim" of our basket on each side of the handle.

Using a paring knife, cut the inside of the skin around the handle of our basket and push the fruit away from the skin.

Remove the fruit from the inside of our basket with your paring knife, and make a small incision at the bottom of the basket to rest our garnish on.

Finally, fill your basket with several pomegranate seeds, and place on the rim of your glass.

Variety is the spice of life!

ORATA AL CARTOCCIO

ORATA AL CARTOCCIO:

Sea Bream in Parchment Paper
4 servings

FOR THE FISH:

2 Sea Bream of 2.5 lbs each (Sea Bream is similar to Sea Bass and can be found in a good fish market. They are red in color and firm in texture. It is the perfect fish to be roasted in the oven with this method. You can also substitute a small Sea Bass or Mullet).

6 Cloves of Garlic
2 Sprigs of Thyme
20 Heirloom Cherry Tomatoes
1 Bunch of Basil
Fleur De Sel
Fresh Ground Black Pepper
4 Lemon
3 Sprigs of Rosemary
1 Egg White

Have your fish guy clean the fish for you - no scales, gutted, and with no gills. Season the fish inside and out with salt, black pepper, rosemary and couple of slices of lemon.

Cut 20 x 16 inches sheet of parchment paper or big enough to hold one fish inside and still have some edge to fold it like an envelope. Before closing it, add around the fish the garlic, the thyme, the peeled cherry tomato, **(for the peeled cherry tomato see the branzino's recipe)** the basil and some more slices of lemon. Drizzle with oil.

Close the paper like a pocket. Brush the edge of the paper with egg white so they will not open in the oven. Preheat the oven at 475 degrees. Place the fish in it and count at least 25/30 minutes for the whole fish, depending also on the thickness. You can, after the time is up, open a side of the bag (be careful is hot) and poke the fish with a skewers to feel if the flesh is done. Open the bag and serve the whole fish in a platter. You can easily separate the flesh from the bones. Drizzle with oil and lemon.

OLD SCHOOL

My brain is the key that sets my mind free.
__Harry Houdini

ZENTINI

1 ½ oz (6 counts) Citrus Vodka
1oz (4 counts) Zen Liqueur
½ oz (2 counts) Sweet & Sour

1 Taro root

PREPARATION:
Fill the shaker with ice; while the shaker is chilling start pouring all the ingredients in the mixing glass. Pour the water off the melted ice and shake vigorously. Stir it into a chilled martini glass.

Light-green with yellow reflections, this cocktail realizes the complex perfume of citrus and herbs.

The intense taste of the vodka dissolves in the warmness of the green tea liqueur.

LA STORIA:
Within all of us lies the power to be the best that we can be! Waking up in the morning, walking down the streets of Ventura or doing yoga in the living room, one can't help but think, "I hope I can stay this grounded all day today." It feels good to relax and unwind, doesn't it? This Zentini is simply the perfect way to get the job done! As the freshness of the citrus fills your mouth and nose, you will feel centered. I'm sure you'll agree that when it comes to a refreshing and relaxing drink, the Zentini reigns supreme.

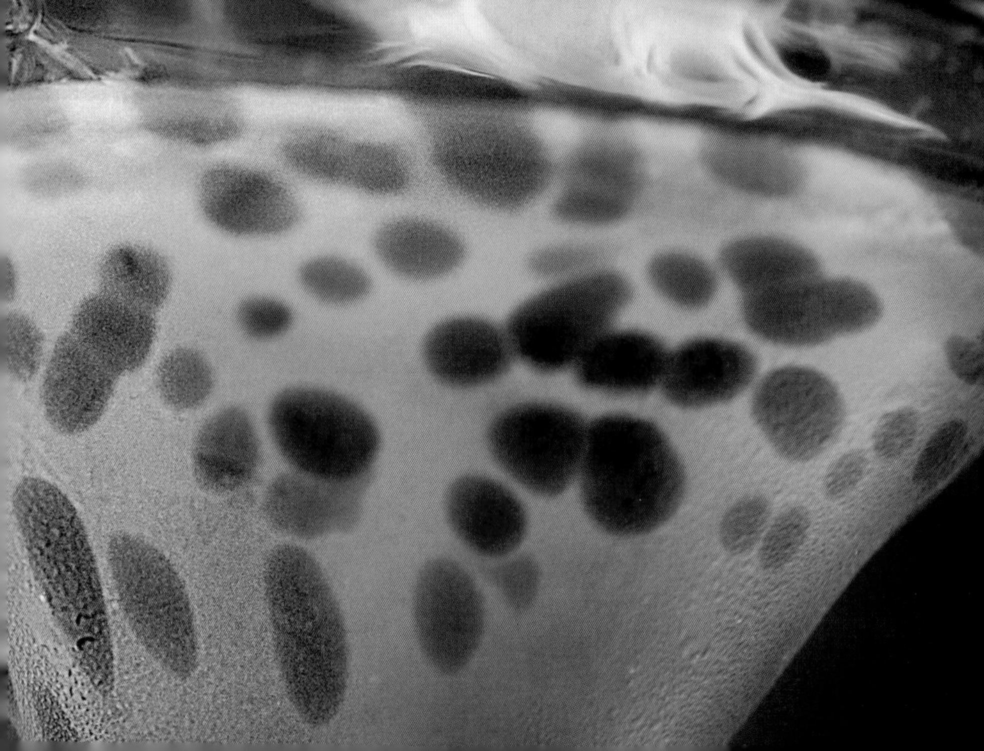

Cut a large circular segment from a taro root to use as a canvas. Using a paring knife, cut a guideline into your canvas, and start your canvas removal by cutting a direct line from the rim down to the top of the "head" then down the shoulders, and finally cut out at the arm.

Continue around the "hand," then into the canvas a bit to the "knee," follow with three equal-length cuts (like the top of a trapezoid) to create the "seat" of the figure.

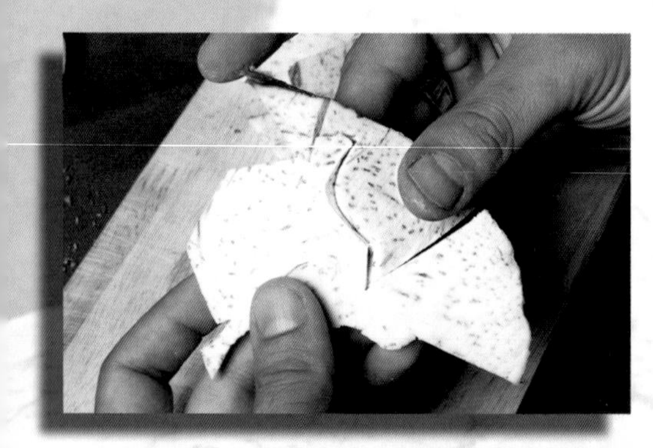

Finish the outline by cutting around the "hand," then back up the "body" to the "neck" of our garnish, then cut and remove the canvas around the top of the head.

Carefully cut small thin wedges, separating the arms from the body and legs.

Very carefully cut small holes into the hands, giving the appearance of the hands in a meditative state, and finally a small incision in the middle of the bottom of the figure to give our garnish a resting place.

Chicken fobia

__Fabio Viviani

In this book as you probably will notice there are no recipes that feature chicken as main focus. I hate chicken. I use to love it...Roasted Chicken, Chicken Parmigiana, Chicken Piccata. I had tons of those things, but here there is something wrong about that little goofy bird. I do chicken at my restaurant because I know where my chickens come from and I know what is going on with the chicken that I buy for my customer. I cannot give you a recipe for a chicken dish and then have you go buy the chicken in some place that I'm not sure that the chicken you will use and feed your kids has been raised properly. That it is not just the effect of some hormone or filled with antibiotics. Sorry, for the chicken recipe maybe I'll see you all at one of my classes or having dinner at my restaurant.

Let me tell you couple of things about your friend: The Chicken.

In Italia the chickens that my family has are free to run behind my house up to the hills of Florence. They eat the grass; they eat all the leftovers from my table. They also eat everything that can be found on the ground and everything that they will like to eat: bugs, leaves from some tree and other stuff that probably fall from the sky.

Every morning I use to get one egg still warm from my little chicken cage where we use to keep the older chicken, the one in charge of the egg production (whoever said that you should not eat more than 2 egg per week? What a fool!) and I think that for the first 9 or 10 years of my life if you don't count maybe just the first year, I've been eating an average of one egg a day, and believe me, all the parameters in my blood are more than perfect (cholesterol what?).

In Italy the chickens are healthy and grow strong because we take care of them. We have to eat them later on of course, so that is why we take such good care of them. They eat as good as we do, they rest as much as they want, they run free as much as they like because sooner or later that happy chicken will be the food for me and my family. I can't afford to feed them bad food because that food will go on my table; I can't allow that on my grandfather's table.

Chicken products, mechanically separated chicken, fried chicken, dumplings, chicken nuggets...I can leave this for the table of someone else's grandfather.

Once in a while, when there was a special occasion, my grandfather would go in our chicken cage and kill the rooster, the biggest chicken in the kingdom, just for special occasion. He would call all of us, the kids in the family, to show us that after cutting the head off a chicken there is some sort of muscular reaction that makes the chicken nerve twitch and the chicken without his head will run for another minute or two. (Where you think that the say "you are running like a chicken with no head" come from? Now you know one thing that my grandfather was saying is also pretty famous in USA). Of course, not having a head caused the chicken to crash against either a wall or against an edge and stop his run. Can you imagine your son coming back to the house and telling you that your neighbor was showing him how to decapitate a chicken...What would you do?

After the decapitation, the chicken was hung by the feet on the porch behind the barn at my house and left to bleed for at least one whole day. The blood was saved in a bucket and with that my grandpa fertilized the soil. He used to tell us that the blood had lots of nutrients good for the plant. The next day the chicken, after being there all this time, was been given to my grandma. She took all the feathers out by hand, burning some of them. After that she gutted the chicken and she kept the neck, the liver, the heart and the feet. She was using them in all kinds of different recipes of our family tradition. Then she got the body ready for the roasting, leaving this in a marinade with all kinds of herbs and submerged with a good olive oil for at least another half day, absolutely outside the refrigerator or the oil will freeze.

The day after the killing and another half day in the mixture with oil and herbs, we were cutting the chicken in quarters and throwing it in a sheet pan in a wood oven probably around 700-800 degrees. At this point the skin was really crispy. My dad was in charge of taking the burning-piping-hot-ash out in order to lower the temperature inside the oven and finish cooking the chicken.

Shame on you if your chicken was fully cooked. You will be sent to jail in that case, the best chicken has to be still a little pink at the bone, especially where the dark meat is, close to the leg. My great grandmother was completely without teeth, so with merely a chicken leg she was acting as if she had a chicken lollipop. She was sucking the leg and chewing the meat out with her gums, and she was cursing at you in case the Chicken was overdone. The worst thing is for the chicken to be just a bit dry (she died in 1987 when she was 96), of course she had no teeth; how the hell would it be possible for her to chew on an overcooked-fully-cooked American-style chicken? You know how she died? Not with some sort of food poisoning or an attack of Salmonella. After having eating for her entire life undercooked meat and still-pink-at-the-bone-chicken, she died because she fell off the stairs after she had a bottle of wine! She used to drink a good glass of wine every day since she was six, probably, and she died happy due to a Hemorrhage as a consequence of the fall. In the last couple of years she would not drink a glass, but more like a bottle, but what you want to tell her; she was telling us to give her a break. Good food and good wine was all she had left.

That chicken, the one that my grandma was craving, was so good and juicy, that my dad and my grandpa were having one whole chicken each and I was eating half of one (I was 9) and I can still remember.

Now, on the other hand let's check the situation we have here about chicken. There are thousands of companies that do chicken products, which means products that feature chicken.

The chickens are not running free in the back yard here. Until last year I was living in this condo in Ventura County, and I was not even able to keep my dog in the house.

If I invite you for dinner at my farmhouse here and you did eat a roasted Chicken, and maybe even like it. Then I tell you that the chicken was kept in my backyard, free to eat whatever...bugs...lizard...and then I tell you that I choke him, cut his head off in front of your kids and I left on the porch bleeding out for two days, out of the refrigerator, (can you imagine your health department?), and then after you have finished eating, I tell you that it was not fully cooked, still a little bit underdone toward the bone, and probably the temperature in the core of the legs did not reach 165 degrees like your safety rules ask for...I'm pretty sure your reaction will be call the police and your lawyer and sue me for attempted murder and for trying to poison you and your family.

I'm not here to scare you. I don't do that in this country. I respect the sanitary rules here (even if some of them seem really silly), and I don't serve undercooked chicken (unless you don't ask me). I just want to inform you in which reality we both, me and my half-brother Jacopo, which unfortunately who is also my partner in the business, grew up in the suburbs of Florence. Our life, without having too much afterthought or too much b***s*** in your head, but always paying respect for whatever you have in your hand; vegetable, fish or meat - it does not matter.

You know what "out of sight out of mind" means? It is the first rule of lots of food companies. They are trying to hide the reality from you and resell it in a different shape or in the way that your brain, devastated with TV publicity and lots of big brand, is gonna like it.

This is what they teach you in the television and in the newspaper, they show you a picture of kids playing happy with a piece of chicken in his hand that due to its shape looks like a gold fish. And the kid is happy to eat the little fish-chicken-what-the-hell-is-that product because the food coloring inside turn the whole things red...how about that?

And then, of course, at my restaurant you pretend the chicken is overcooked, the fish with no bone, the shrimp without heads and the seafood linguini without the shell - what? The fish has bones in it? The shrimp has an actual head? Of course, that thing was alive couple of days ago. Do you know what they do in Italy when the fish is start to be kind of old, they take the head off, the bone out and they marinate the filet in oil, garlic and pepper and they sell this to the tourist at the market.

This is the reason why I order just whole fish at the restaurant, unless I'm not having dinner at Le-Bernardine or at Craft in New York or in few other high-class restaurants where I know the chef. Where I can trust a fish that is been portioned for me already. If you find a bone in your whole baked sea bass, spit it out or put it to the side with a fork. Don't call the server and complain because you had a little bone on your plate.

As a customer, you have to respect the effort of those trying to make your night a better place to be. Give your server or chef a break, relax and enjoy the ride. Those shrimp, they are not looking at you, they are dead, and the reason why? Somebody killed them because you ordered them. So what the difference if there is the head or not, you order the crime, now you want to feel sorry for them? Shrimp have heads; fish have bones; the steak is rare...period, but it won't kill you (if it is well done, may the chef will). Moist and juice chicken very little pink on the bone will not let you die by a salmonella attack...this is a matter of fact, so learn it and enjoy the dinner.

For Valentine's Day last year at the shopping center behind my house there were heart-shaped chicken nuggets and they where red in color like a stoplight! What is that? Are you people serious?

Let's step back for one second and talk about our chicken friend again. Here you can't breed chicken in your back-yard; the chicken can be fatal for your health. Chicken is a dirty animal and if you touch a chicken you can die of dys-entery; you eat the chicken raw you will die with a salmonella infection (who the hell eat raw chicken anyway?). The chicken is the most dangerous in the animal world, way more dangerous than lion and tiger according to the media. I know people that lost friends because a chicken came in their home at night and kill them all. Do you believe me?

For how many more years will you let the media mess with your brain, trying to sell you fully cooked, natural flavored, mechanically separated pieces of chicken?

For how many years will you let these people tell you what is good and what is not for your health? My grandma she was eating chicken pink at the bone for 90 years and she died falling down the stairs. I'm not saying that starting tomor-row you have to start eating raw chicken but I'm telling you like another famous chef said once that your body is not a temple, it is an amusement park. Don't live inside a glass jar, especially if someone else did the glass for you. Try to go a little bit back to basics; try to utilize healthier food and get your hands a little dirty in the backyard. This is the way I have to do it every day. I'm not Pavarotti or some famous singer that I can put my work of the day in a CD and sell it, living off of it. I have to please you every day or I will find my ass with the rest of my body attached in the middle of a street.

Once in a while some chicken comes back to the kitchen because is too moist and they think is still raw. Some of my customers think that the chicken has to be dry in order to be safely-fully-cooked. Please, get the hell out of my place; leave us alone with the good customers, the ones that understand the effort that we put in every plate we make. That makes us try to be better every day, better than the day before. You know, the person who sends the chicken back to me is the person that goes to eat, on a regular basis, to fast food and loves junk food. It is the person that at midnight goes for a burger with French fries and a Soda filled with sugar and then go to bed. It is the father or the mother of the little kids in television with the chicken nugget shaped like a gold fish in his hand.

Try to read in the back of the box the ingredient label; there are over 30 ingredient and just 3 belong to the food chain.When somewhere you read "Ingredient for the chicken nuggets: chicken 35%," means that just 35% of what's in your mouth is chicken, all the rest is chemical crap, that all it does is make you sick. You are eating this crap for years and then you go to the gym because you are out of shape. Listen to me and start a little vegetable field in that big size backyard that you have. Take off the barbecue you just used for 4 of July, get a shovel and get back to work on your health a little bit.

You complain to me because I'm trying to give you the food in the way it should be eaten (I'm not talking just about chicken) and you miss the big picture. Isn't the fact that I refuse to overcook my meat because it will make you sick the rest of your day and then if you come here and order a well done steak or chicken of course you will get it, but I'm happy? Not really! It is good for you? Not really!

I try to buy the best of the best - organic chicken, free range and organic product. We have our farmer that does grow everything for us in the best way, the old one. He doesn't pump my vegetables with fertilizer. The one who does the chicken for me doesn't pump them with cortisone and when the chicken is almost dead, because medicine doesn't belong to his diet, keep him alive with antibiotics in order to cure the disorder create by the cortisone.

Screw all this things, eat healthy and trust your Chef. He is out there picking the best for you, and if your chicken is still moist and little underdone at the bone it is not because somebody is trying to kill you but because that is the way to do it – My Grandma's way!

CARNE / MEAT

MEAT

by Fabio

The subject of this chapter in Italian culture is huge. Meat is all over Italy, and is a big part of our cuisine. All kinds of meat: beef, pork, lamb, veal, and all kinds of bird and game, all kinds of animal, even horse, rabbit and elk.

Depending where you are in Italy, you will find a piece of meat that is going to resemble the tradition of the town where you have your meal. We don't have the concept of going to the Mega Store with a meat section and picking our meat in between 30 different pre-pack-ready-to-go pieces selected by some butcher that not only you never see but also you never talk to him. When I buy meat in my hometown, it is always a journey. I hang out with my butcher in Florence almost every day, we are not only friends, but I call him when I have some request and he calls me when he has something special that he want me to try. It is the personal relationship, the friendship, that is missing in this country between working with food and people that have to buy it.

Unless you find a single owner butcher shop in your town you will not find any special treatment when you will need that piece of meat that is going to make it or break it you party with your friend at your house.

The selection of meat that you find in each of these huge markets is a good average, almost never dry-aged, but there is way better stuff out there. You just need to get out of your house or Google it up and find where you are able to actually talk to a butcher and not pick out of a supermarket basket.

I can't help it...I love meat. I will eat meat anywhere, anytime, with anyone, each single bit gives me the same great emotion, bigger than any piece of fish, lobster and existing vegetable or food group available. I can be miserable if on my table in my dinner there is not a single piece of meat. Even if people tell me that eating too much meat is dangerous, I don't care. I'm healthy and I see meat through rose-colored glasses. I love it too much in order to give myself another option.

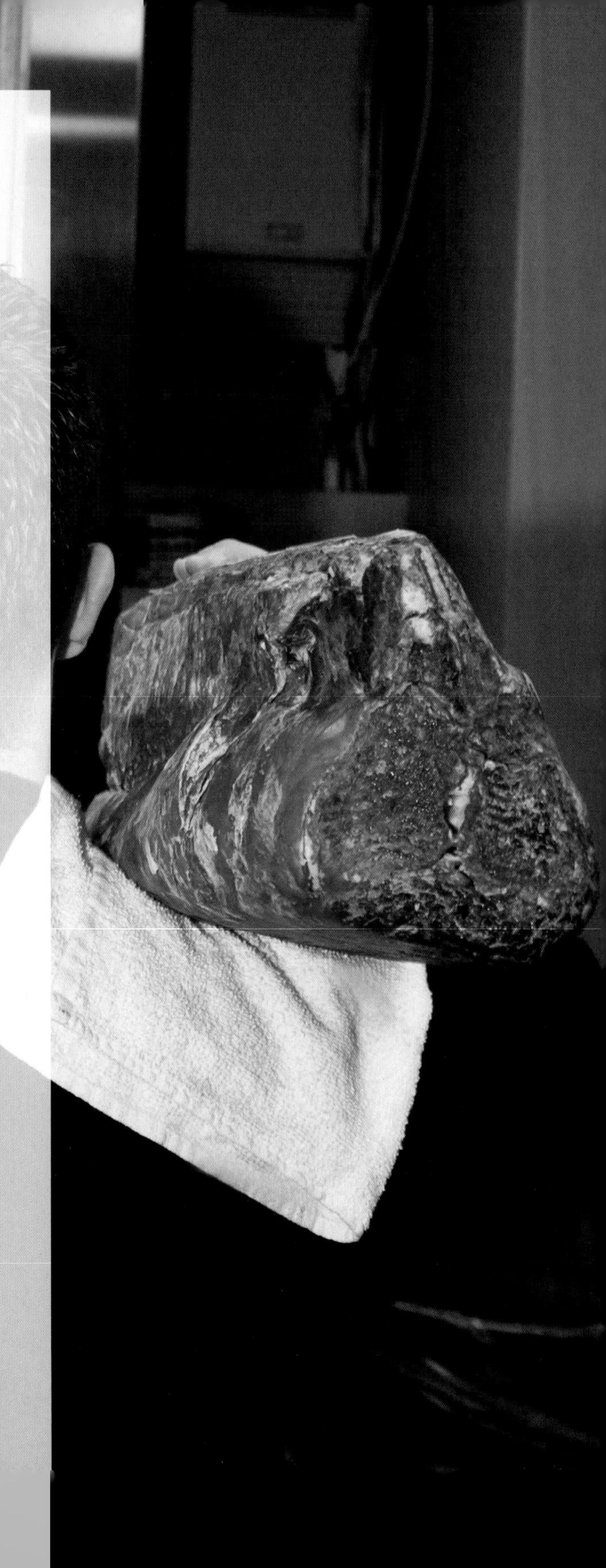

Santa Margherita Chianti Classico is a fruit forward wine, created in the authentic Italian style from the

ABBACCHIO DI AGNELLO ALLA ROMANA CON LE CIPOLLINE:

Baby Lamb with Cipollini Roman Style
4 servings

FOR THE LAMB:
1 C of Extra Virgin Olive Oil
6/7 Cloves of Garlic
2 Sprigs of Rosemary
1 lb of Cipollini Onion
Kosher salt
Fresh Ground Black Pepper
2 C of Dry White Wine
1 Bunch of Mint
8 oz of Pine nuts
5 lbs Bone-in Lamb Shoulder (ask to your Butcher to cut the Meat in 2 inch pieces) or 4 Single Lamb Shank (Hindshank)
Flour for dust
The zest of 2 lemons minced

In a large deep pan, combine the olive oil and the garlic cloves. Put on low fire. Peel the cipollini and add them to the garlic that has been cooking, till both are light golden brown. Once cooked, set them aside. In the same pan with another bit of oil start to cook the lamb lightly dusted with flour and well seasoned with the salt and pepper on medium high heat till it is nicely browned on both sides. Add again the cipollini and garlic mixture, the rosemary, the wine and the pine nuts. Reduce the fire to low and set a piece of aluminum foil directly on top of the meat. Keep cooking and turning the meat till it is tender (1½ hours). You may need to add a little water to keep the sauce from drying out. When cooking, mix the minced lemon zest with the chopped mint and sprinkle on the lamb. Serve family style in a big platter.

Savor your life. Like a good wife, and a fine wine.
___Anonymous

Something that is well done is always better than something that is well said.

__Anonymous

GINGER SERENITY

1½ oz (6 counts) Gin
1 oz (4 counts) Pineapple Puree
½ oz (2 counts) Ginger Syrup
8 to 12 Mint Leaves
2 Tsp of brown sugar
2 Lime wedges

1 Watermelon

PREPARATION:

In a mixing glass muddle the mint with the lime wedges and the brown sugar. Once you make a uniform pulp, add all the ingredients listed in the recipe. Fill your shaker with ice, shake it hard and strain into a chilled Martini glass.

A nice touch will be to add at the bottom green mint liquor to create the nice contrast in color as the picture shows.

The color is light yellow with green specks; the smell is of tropical fruits; the taste is pretty dry, fresh and quenching, with unique aroma and juniper berry scent.

LA STORIA:

The concept of Serenity conjures up an Eastern feeling that would always include Ginger. Ginger has for centuries been used in the Orient for a sense of well being. It is an amazing food and is made into an amazing drink here! We have combined tequila, ginger, ginger root and lime....Yes, it is a great contradiction, but also very beautiful at the same time. Ah, the beauty of contradiction!

Using a decent sized watermelon skin canvas and a paring knife, carefully cut a stencil of your "cat" into the canvas. As before, the best way to start removing excess skin is by cutting from a large cut (in this case, the center of the cat's back).

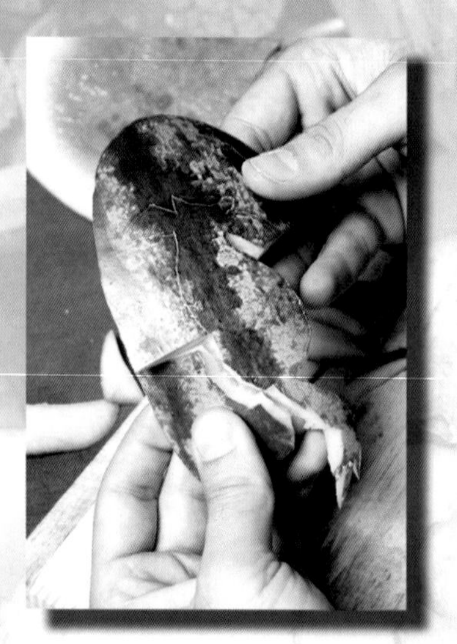

Cut down along the "back" of the cat and remove using a diagonal cut just above the tail.

Shape a cut around the cat's tail all the way up to the center of his front, cutting out from the canvas half way if necessary.

Carefully cut arc shaped whiskers (three on each side should do) from both sides of the cat's head. Finally make a small incision where the front of the cat and the tail meet to give us our resting place for the garnish.

Now cut the head of the cat out from the canvas leaving large triangle shaped pieces on each side of the head which we will use next to form the whiskers.

When I sell liquor, it's called bootlegging; when my patrons serve it on Lake Shore Drive, it's called hospitality.

__Al Capone

PICCIONE AI FUNGHI ARROSTO E PATATE:

Squab with roasted Potato and Mushrooms
4 servings

FOR THE ROASTED MUSHROOMS SAUCE:

8 oz Chanterelle mushrooms
8 oz Oyster mushrooms
8 cloves of Garlic
Kosher Salt
1 lb of Butter
8 oz Hen of Wood mushrooms
3 sprigs of Thyme
1 sprig of Rosemary
Crushed Black Peppercorns
½ C of dry white wine

Clean the dirt from the mushrooms at the bottom and cut them in 3-4 pieces each. Blanch them in boiling water separating them for type. Each mushroom has a different timing of blanching and you can feel it from touching the head and the stem. If spongy they will blanch faster, if firm they will take more time because it won't absorb water as fast as the other one. Once done set them in a dry towel. Melt half of the butter with the thyme inside and the crushed garlic and the rosemary.

Let the butter and herbs go for 6-8 minutes on medium fire, add the mushrooms and bring the fire to high. When the edge of the mushrooms are getting a nice brown color is time to add salt and fresh crushed pepper to the mushrooms, deglaze with the wine and let them still cook for another 5 minutes.

FOR THE POTATOES:

1 lb of Kennebec or Russet Potato
Kosher Salt
½ C of olive Oil
1 C of Sage Leaf
8 Cloves of garlic
Fresh Ground Pepper
4 sprigs of Rosemary

Peel the potato and cut it in one inch squares, boil them in water till they are soft enough to be able to be cut in half with a butter knife, drain them and place them in a sheet pan, drizzle with all the oil. Add a good amount of salt and fresh ground pepper, peel and roughly chop the garlic, clean the rosemary and coarsely chop the sage. Add everything to the potatoes and roast them in the oven at 400 degrees till the outside is crispy and brown, place the potatos on the bottom, the Squab on top of the potato and finish with the mushrooms.

FOR THE SQUAB:

4 Squab butterflied (ask your butcher to do it for you) and Flattened (you can be substitute with Poussin or Cornish game but cooking time will slightly change)
¼ C of Balsamic Vinegar
1 Clove of Garlic Minced
1 Tbsp of Fresh ground Pepper
1 Tbsp of chopped Sage
2 Tbsp of Olive Oil
3 each of Green Onion finely chopped
1Tbsp of chopped Rosemary
½ lb unsalted butter

Combine all the ingredients and use this liquid to marinate the Squab for at least 3 Hours. In the meantime get ready the remaining component of the plate, at the end the Squab will take just few minutes to cook. When ready, place them on the very hot grill skin down for 8 minutes, turn them and add salt and pepper. The Squab has to be medium Rare at the bone in the breast to be perfect, let them cook on the other side for 4-5 minutes, serve them sitting on the potato with the mushrooms on top. Add fresh pepper and olive oil. Put the marinade in a sauté pan and reduce to half, add the butter and keep reducing till smooth and velvety. The sauce should not be watery or runny. Strain and drizzle the squab once cooked.

An old girlfriend once told me that men are like pumpkins. All the good ones had either been taken, or had everything scraped out of their heads with a spoon.

__Jacopo Falleni

WASABI MARTINI

1½ oz (6 counts) Vodka or pepper vodka
¾ oz (3 counts) fresh squeeze lemon juice
¾ oz (3 counts) simple syrup or ginger syrup
1 pea of wasabi paste

1 Pumpkin

PREPARATION:
Place the wasabi paste in a mixing glass. Pour the simple syrup (see glossary) and the lemon juice and with a mixing spoon gently stir and add the Vodka. Fill the shaker with ice and shake it briskly, then strain it into a frozen martini glass.

This is very spicy! The drink is opaque green with a unique and strong nose. The mouth has a simultaneous sensation of fiery wasabi and refreshing lemon.

All of the ingredients in this recipe are useful to cleanse your palate. That's why this drink is the perfect pairing for fish based dishes.

LA STORIA:

For Italians, when you think of spicy, you think of passion. The spice of wasabi makes this drink almost an aphrodisiac.

This time we will use a bit of a different canvas. Take a pumpkin and remove a large piece of skin from one side (a large knife may be necessary, pumpkin skin can be a little tough!).

Using a paring knife, cut guidelines around a stencil of our pumpkin "vulture."

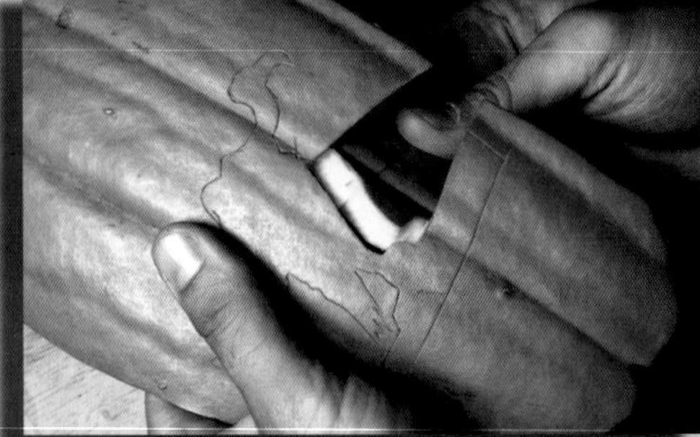

Cut into the canvas to the bottom of the small ruffle under our vulture's "neck," down along the front to the "perch" then out.

Now, from the top of the cut out, form the ruffle, up the neck, around the "beak" and "head" of the vulture, continuing down the back of the neck and cut out at the "shoulder." Continue again down to the bottom of the "wing."

Cut out the canvas around the back of the tail, up to the legs and around the left side of the perch, and remove the underside of the canvas from the perch.

Using the tip of your paring knife cut a VERY small, triangular shaped wedge from the center of the head to give the appearance of an evil eye which will add to the character of our garnish. Lastly making a diagonal incision to the perch under the "legs" to give our garnish its resting place.

Delicate bubbles and hints of apple and peach make Santa Margherita Prosecco perfect as an aperitif, or with lighter fare, such as seafood and delicate risotto.

FILETTO DI MAIALE ALLA CAMOMILLA CON SPINACI ALLA CREMA

FILETTO DI MAIALE ALLA CAMOMILLA CON SPINACI ALLA CREMA:
Chamomile encrusted Pork Tenderloin with creamed Spinach
4 servings

FOR THE SPINACH:

1 stick of butter
1 C of half and half
1 Tbsp of Fresh Ground Pepper
1 Nutmeg
½ Tsp of Baking Soda
¼ C of Flour
1 Tbsp Salt
1.5 Lbs of fresh Spinach
2 oz of Cream cheese
2 oz of Parmesan cheese

In a saucepan over medium heat start the butter and let it melt, add the salt and the pepper for taste and add the flour. Turn the fire off and mix well, add the half and half and turn the fire back on low. Keep stirring until the mixture starts to thicken. Now add the cream Cheese, set aside once fully incorporated. Bring to boil a pot of water and add the baking soda. Once it is boiling put all the spinach inside and let cook till the spinach is completely wilted (about 4 minutes); strain the spinach and with the help of a towel squeeze the water out. Place the spinach in the creamy sauce and let them cook on medium for another 5 minutes, grate the cheese and add it at the end.

FOR THE PORK:

2 Whole Pork Tenderloin
10 bags of Chamomile Tea
Fresh Ground Pepper
1 C of Breadcrumb, finely minced
Salt
1 Egg White

Preheat the grill, in a food processor blend the breadcrumbs, a tbsp. of salt, some fresh pepper. Open the chamomile tea and mix into the breadcrumbs.

Whisk the egg white with little bit of water and brush the whole tenderloin. Heavily season with salt and pepper, roll the tenderloin in the bread/chamomile mixture making sure that the whole tenderloin is nicely coated with the crumbs. Place on the hot grill turning the meat so you will have even grill marks. Grill for a period of 6/8 minutes, let the meat rest for 5 minutes so the juice will be redistributed. Preheat the oven to 400 and place the tenderloin in it for another 5 minutes. Slice 2 inches thick and place cut face up on the spinach.

PRODOTTI TIPICI
PANINI
CIACCINI
PIZZE

CHAMOMILE MARTINI

1 ½ oz (6 counts) Vanilla Rum
1 ½ oz (6 counts) St. Germaine Liqueur
½ oz (2 counts) Sweet and Sour

1 Taro root
1 Pineapple

PREPARATION:
Fill a Cocktail shaker with ice. Add the rum, St. Germaine Liqueur and Sweet and Sour (see glossary). Shake vigorously. Strain into a chilled and chamomile tea rimmed martini glass.

For the rim, mix a bag of chamomile tea with granulated sugar and dip your glass into it...mmm!

Light in color, the cocktail has a nice strong perfume that switches from herbaceous nose to fresh fruit flavors. The taste is warm and off-dry, giving a long hug of the aromas of Elderflowers and vanilla. This leaves a sweet essence of chamomile in the mouth.

LA STORIA
This drink is very sweet and with the Chamomile, is very relaxing. A good night's sleep can sometimes best be achieved with a good nightcap. What is more perfect for a good rest than Chamomile and rum? The flavor is reminiscent of a nice evening off...are you ready for sweet dreams?

Nature does not hurry,
yet everything is accomplished.
__Lao Tzu

To create the center of our "flower," we must first cut off the top half of a pineapple.

Using a melon ball scoop remove the center of the pineapple.

Next, cut a circular segment from a taro root approximately an eighth inch thick.

Take a "tear drop" cookie cutter, and remove 6 identical pieces from the canvas, giving us the "petals" for our flower.

Layer each petal on top of another, then with a toothpick, pierce through the middle of the stack about a quarter inch from the pointed tip.

Finally take the pineapple ball and pierce about half way through with the end of the toothpick so the pick does not go all the way through the ball, and rest on top of your martini in between the top and bottom petal.

Three things I crave: good food, good drinks, and good hospitality.
__Danny Meyer

LA BISTECCA PERFETTA

LA BISTECCA PERFETTA:
The perfect Rib Eye
4 servings

FOR THE STEAK:
4 each Prime Cut Rib Eye 22 oz each (at Least), best if dry aged.
1 Tbs of chopped Rosemary
1 Tbs of chopped Sage
Fresh Ground Black Pepper
4 Cloves of Garlic with the skin on
2 Meyer Lemons
½ C Extra Virgin Olive Oil
2 Sprigs of Thyme
½ C of kosher salt
Fresh Ground Pepper

Place the oil in a Sauté pan with the garlic and the thyme. Cook on low till the garlic can be easily smashed and comes out from the skin. Smash the garlic to a paste and at this point strain so you will have the scented oil plus a little juice from the garlic. Keep the oil aside in the refrigerator.

The meat has to be room temperature before being cooked. Season the meat with the herbs and the pepper. It is a good thing that you don't salt the meat until one side is cooked (the salt will start to absorb the juice of the meat). The grill has to be really hot and the meat nice and coated with the herbs, lots of herbs, Grill on one side, after 5 minutes turn the meat on the other side, and again 1 time for each side, let the meat rest for at least another 5 minutes, during the grilling you can add salt as you go, and at the end drizzle with the scented olive oil, cut the lemon in half and grill it for a couple of minutes, grilling the lemon will bring out the sweetness, serve with olive oil and the lemon on the side.

Being from Florence, I know there is just one thing to drink when you are having a steak, a great glass of wine. So, this time...no martini!

I know my wines and I have a personal favorite. May I say that under the rolling hills of Tuscany, there is a small set of vineyards (maybe 125 hectares) owned by a man named Lavinio Franceschi. Of his five Tuscan red wines, I must say that Brunello is by far the best. I find it to taste very young and I highly recommend it! It has a full, fresh body with 100% hand-picked Sangiovese fruit, about 13% alcohol, and aged about three years in French Oak barrels. Many wine experts in Italia feel that the 1997 Brunello di Montalcino, Il Poggione is the best since 1947. Do yourself a favor, my friends, and grab a bottle while you can and treat you and your guests to a savory storm of flavor that could only come from under the Tuscan sun! At home, I would wonder how big the world really was! I wanted to see everything. I wanted to know people from every country and every walk of life. I felt like the more things we shared, the closer we would become as a people and a world. I love this country and love sharing with my friends here those things that I have come across in my globetrotting (and by the way, I can't play basketball to save my life!) But remember, this is my land; of olive oil, and the godfather; so I bring to you a gift from my land, a gift from a far place, my Bella Italia!

MARCA
PROPRIA
TENUTA "GREPPO"
FRANCO BIONDI SANTI
MONTALCINO-ITALIA

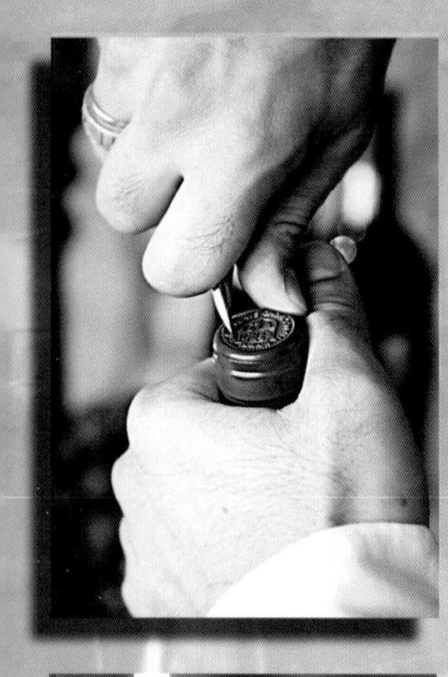

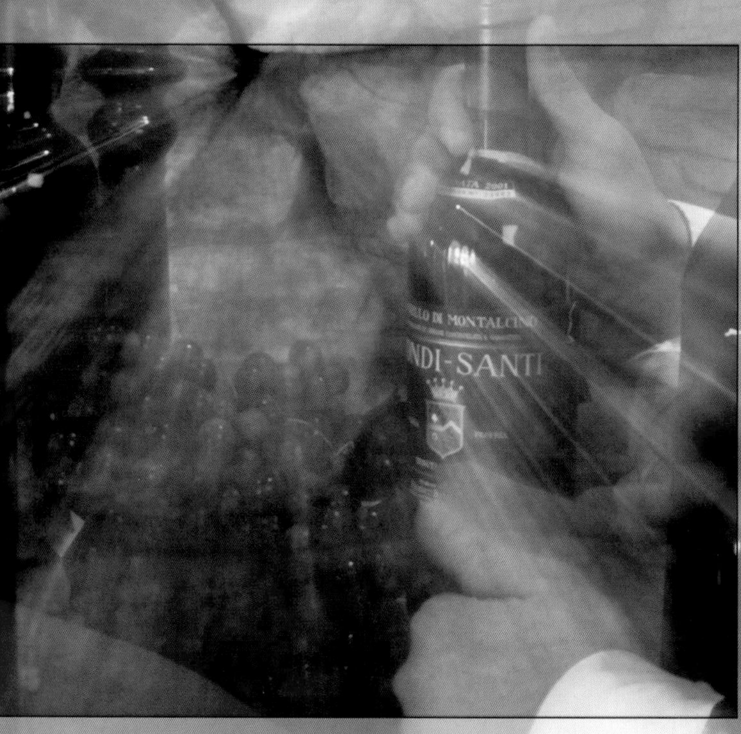
LLO DI MONTALCINO
NDI-SANTI

DOLCI - DESSERTS

DESSERT

by Fabio

Italians are not big in dessert...we are no French! We don't need to make lasting impression because our meal was average! I am just kidding, I love and respect French cuisine. No really, I'm kidding! But it is true we are not a nation of dessert-professionals. But, the few things that we do, like gelato and sorbet are some pretty bad boy desserts! And homemade Tart and Pies are pretty hard to match by any other culture also.

America is trying to steal our gelato, putting up a way cheaper, less healthy version called Ice cream, which is nasty to me, ok there are some good brands of Ice Cream that I actually like, but nothing like a homemade Gelato, sorry fellas, there is not competition.

My mom bakes those two or three things in the house like Apple pie or Tiramisu. Most of the time if you need a dessert in Italy for your family or you want to bring a dessert to someone's house you will go and buy a good dessert from some pasticceria that makes dessert and only does that. The desserts in this book are some of the most traditional in Italy and also have some French influence (I told you I don't have problem with French). I really do want to give a little credit to France too...at the end, they are not so bad, and even if the Traditional French cuisine was born after our Queen moved to France couple of Century back and married one of the Famous-then French King, bringing with her the recipes and tradition of the regional Italian cuisine, they did some good stuff to in the past, so I will be kind and give them credit.

TIRAMISU DELLA MIA NONNA:
My Grand Mother Tiramisu
Serves 10/12 people

5 lbs Mascarpone
12 egg yolks
11 oz sugar
1QT Heavy Cream
4 C of espresso Coffee

Whip the cream with 1/2 the sugar. Set aside. Whisk egg yolks and the rest of the sugar until light in color. Spoon in the mascarpone and mix thoroughly, scraping down the sides often. Finally, add the whipped cream and mix all together until just combined. Mixture will thicken while refrigerated.

Use ladyfingers soaked in espresso to layer between cream, and dust in shaved chocolate.

Because making a moment perfect is better than making a profit.

__Anonymous

ESPRESSOTINI

¾ oz or (3 counts) Vanilla Vodka
½ oz or (2 counts) Baileys Irish Cream
½ oz or (2 counts) Kahlua
1 Shot of Espresso (chilled)
¼ oz or (1counts) Whipped Cream

PREPARATION:

First step...Make a nice cup of espresso. Once you have that.... drink it! Because if you are like me you will not be able to resist it!

Jokes a side... pour into the mixing glass the ingredient following the recipes. Shake it well and strain it into a chilled chocolate rimmed and chocolate drizzled martini glass or cognac balloon.

This drink is indicated for a long, cold winter night. The color is very inviting; the aroma is of fresh cream with light fragrance of vanilla.

The pleasure found in sipping this drink comes from a delicate and balanced combination of strong coffee flavors and smooth yet rich interaction between the liquor and the cream.

LA STORIA:

I am an espresso addict! If there was a twelve-step program for espresso I would have to go! This having been said, it is clear that I truly love this drink. Now, can I have a double?

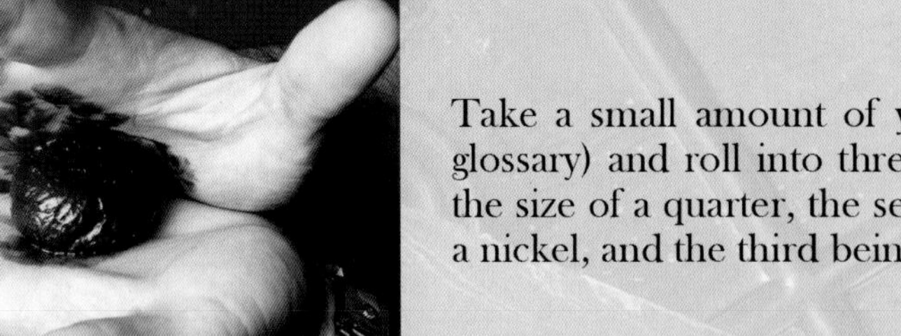

Take a small amount of your chocolate ganache (see glossary) and roll into three balls, the first being about the size of a quarter, the second being about the size of a nickel, and the third being about the size of a dime.

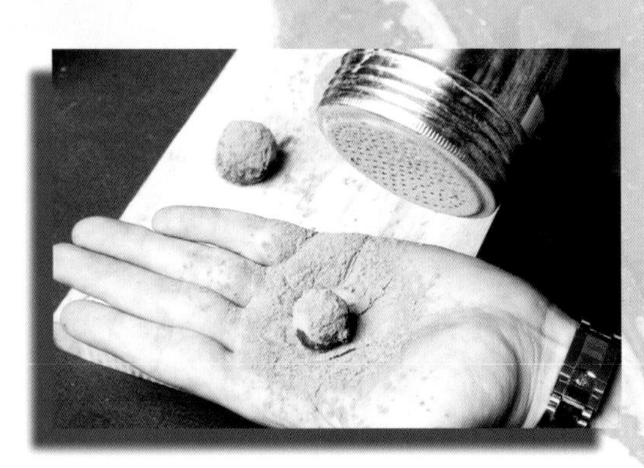

Dust each ganache ball with a fair coat of chocolate powder.

Take a nice garnish pick (preferably a 5 inch prism) and pierce all the way through the largest ball.

Continue with the medium sized ball, and finish with the smallest ball. Use the lip between the large and medium ball to rest your garnish on the rim of the glass.

We work to become, not to acquire!
__Albert Hubbard

DOLCE AL CIOCCOLATO SENZA FARINA:

Flourless Chocolate cake with Coffee Cream Anglaise
Makes about 14 little cakes

12 egg yolks (separate the whites in another bowl)
1½ C granulated sugar
2 Tbsp Brandy
3 Tbsp vanilla extract
2 lbs melted chocolate
¾ lb melted butter
1/3 C sugar

FOR THE CHOCOLATE CAKE:

Combine melted butter and chocolate in a bowl, set aside. Whisk egg yolks with 1 ½ cups of sugar, brandy, and vanilla, set aside. Whip egg whites in mixer with 1/3 cup of sugar. Mix chocolate mixture with the yolks, then finally egg white mixture. Pour into well greased ramekins.

Bake at 325 for approximately 22 min. Allow to cool for about 15 min and remove from ramekin. Dust with powdered sugar.

FOR THE COFFEE CREAM:

½ qt half and half
½ qt heavy cream
9 egg yolks
1 ¼ C sugar
½ C toasted coffee beans

Whip eggs and sugar, set aside. Combine cream and half and half, bring to a boil. Turn off heat and quickly whisk in egg mixture. Return to heat, stirring constantly until mix begins to boil. Remove from heat and stir in coffee beans. Allow to cool at least two hours infusing coffee beans. Strain before use.

VANILLA BEAN GELATO:

2 C of Milk
1 C Heavy Cream
4 Eggs Yolk
½ C of Sugar
3 Vanilla Beans

Boil the milk and the cream together, one bring to boil, add the vanilla beans, whisk it and let cool down for 30 minutes. Whip the egg yolks with the sugar until they double in volume, add the milk mixture little by little and the strain, bring to boil again until the mixture coats the back of a wooden spoon, let cool down and place it in an ice cream maker and process according to manufacture direction.

MART

DOLCE DE LECHE

1 ½ oz (or 6 counts) Vanilla Vodka
½ oz (or 2 counts) Godiva Caramel Liqueur
½ oz (or 2 counts) Baileys Irish Cream
¼ oz (or 1 counts) Whipped Cream

PREPARATION:

Fill the shaker with ice. Add the Vodka and the Caramel Liqueur, the Irish cream and the cream, shake briskly. Strain into a chilled graham cracker rimmed martini glass; garnish and serve.

The presence of the cream influences the color and the smell. The taste is initially warm and becomes creamy and rounded leaving a long and persistent caramel sensation in the mouth.

LA STORIA

Ah, la dolce vita! It means the good life! How wonderful life can be with all its opportunities to try new things. Now, look! Here you have added a brand new recipe to your own personal repertoire of alternatives to the usual lineup of martini suspects. The Dolce le Leche will always stand out and is actually completely appropriate for any occasion from casual lunches to your next black tie event!

Hold a crystal pick flat while you take a large dripping spoonful of our sugar mixture (see glossary).

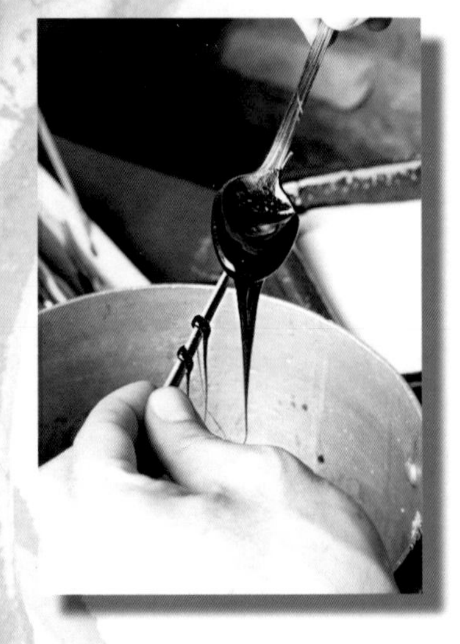

Using circular motions with your "spoon hand," wrap the drizzling sugar around the stationary crystal pick.

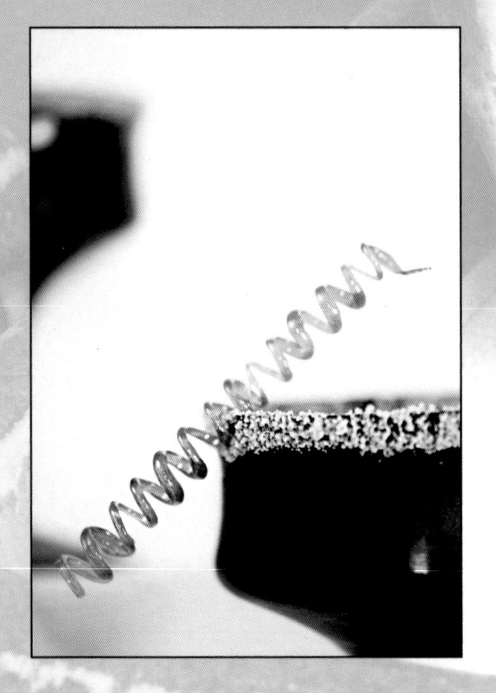

Continue to the end of the pick, and once at the end, use the neck of your spoon to collect the drippings off each spiral.

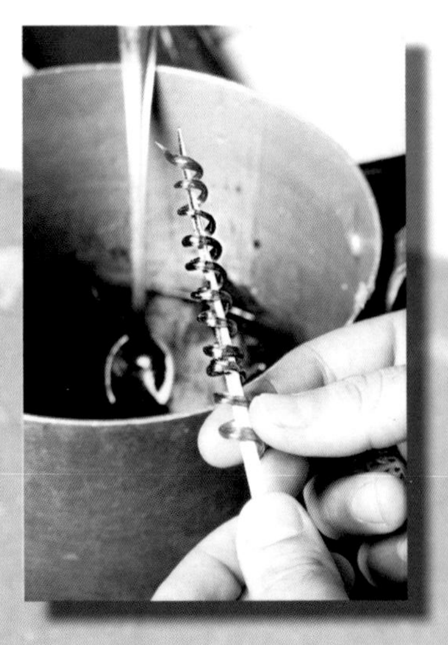

Once dry, simply slip the sugar spiral off the crystal pick and rest the center of the spiral on your glass.

Friends are not there only in times of need, they are there always.

__Anonymous

TRIO DI CREMA:
Trio of Creme Brulee, Vanilla Bean, Chai Spices, Espresso

FOR THE VANILLA CRÈME BRULEE:
3 C heavy cream
1 ½ C milk
1 ½ whole vanilla beans
9 egg yolks
¾ C sugar

Bring heavy cream, milk, and beans (cut in half lengthwise) to a boil. In mixer, whisk yolks and sugar until light and fluffy. Turn off heat on cream and slowly pour about half of cream into egg yolks while whisking. Quickly whisk egg mixture into remaining cream. Strain. Divide among ramekins. Bake in a hotel pan (or an oven safe dish with high sides) with water filled about half way up the sides of the ramekins. Cover the container tightly in foil. Bake at 275, check in 25 min.

FOR THE CHAI SPICES CRÈME BRULEE:
3 C heavy cream
1 ½ C milk
10 oz loose chai tea
9 egg yolks
1 C sugar

Bring heavy cream, milk, and chai tea to a boil; continue to heat on a low simmer until liquid is a light brown color. In mixer, whisk yolks and sugar until light and fluffy. Turn off heat on cream and slowly pour about half of cream into egg yolks while whisking. Quickly whisk egg mixture into remaining cream. Strain through a fine mesh strainer to remove the tea leaves. Divide among ramekins. Bake in a hotel pan (or an oven safe dish with high sides) with water filled about half way up the sides of the ramekins. Cover the container tightly in foil. Bake at 275, check in 25 min.

FOR THE ESPRESSO CRÈME BRULEE:
3 C heavy cream
1 ½ C milk
1 ½ C coffee extract
9 egg yolks
1 ¼ C sugar

Bring heavy cream, milk, and coffee extract to a boil; continue to heat on a low simmer until liquid is a light brown color. In mixer, whisk yolks and sugar until light and fluffy. Turn off heat on cream and slowly pour about half of cream into egg yolks while whisking. Quickly whisk egg mixture into remaining cream. Divide among ramekins. Bake in a hotel pan (or an oven safe dish with high sides) with water filled about half way up the sides of the ramekins. Cover the container tightly in foil. Bake at 275, check in 25 min.

To live is the rarest thing in the world. Most people exist, that is all.

__Oscar Wilde

BANANA CHAI MARTINI

1 ½ oz (6 counts) Coconut Rum
½ oz (2 counts) Crème de Banana
½ oz (2 counts) White Godiva Liqueur
½ oz (2 counts) Chai Syrup
¼ oz (1 count) Whipped Cream

PREPARATION:

Pour all the ingredients in a mixing glass exactly as the recipe says. Fill the shaker with ice. Shake it strongly and serve it in chilled martini glass. Make sure the glass has been decorated with a sugar drizzle before you pour.

The color is white with caramel riffles and has the smell of fresh cream and chai. The taste is warm, sweet, very soft and gently creamy with a finish full of banana aroma.

LA STORIA:

I truly believe that my job is a lifestyle. And, moreover, a lifestyle that is not for everyone. The two most important things about my work are easy. First, don't be afraid to work long hours. Second, make every one of your customers feel special! We all love to feel special. It is my honor to make you feel that way when you walk through the door of Café Firenze.

For this garnish, we will use the same sugar mixture from the Dolce De Leche martini. (see glossary).

Take a 6 oz ladle and turn it so the bottom of the ladle is facing up. Take a large spoonful of the sugar mixture and drizzle consecutive parallel lines across the ladle.

Continue drizzling parallel lines in three different directions, then a few curved drizzles here and there to add texture.

Once dry, remove the "sugar cap" from the bottom of the ladle and place directly on top of your martini glass.

With the same sugar you can also decorate the inside of your glass like the picture shows.

DonQ
DonQ
GOLD
Produced by
Serrallés, Inc. Ponce, Puerto Rico
DonQ

PANNA COTTA CON LE FRAGOLE:
Cooked Cream with Balsamic Strawberries

3 C heavy cream
21 diced strawberries
1 C whole milk
3 C balsamic vinegar
½ C sugar
2 C granulated sugar
1 Tbsp vanilla extract
1 C of Pureed Strawberry (just blend 1 cup of strawberry with a little water)
1 Tsp lemon zest
½ oz unflavored gelatin (four sheets)

FOR THE CREAM GELATIN:
In a bowl bloom gelatin with milk, combine cream and sugar and heat in a saucepan until bubbles appear around the edges. Add lemon zest and vanilla, add the cream to the milk and whisk. Strain and Divide among ramekins or glassware. To serve from ramekin, set in hot water, run a knife around the edge and turn out into dish.

FOR BALSAMIC STRAWBERRIES:
Whisk the sugar gradually into the balsamic vinegar (grains of sugar may remain at bottom of mix, either strain mix or heat on stove top until melted.) Stir in some of the strawberry pureed until flavor is well balanced and desirable. Pour over the diced strawberries, and topped onto the gelatin.

You know you're in love when you can't fall asleep because reality is finally better than the dreams!
__Dr. Seuess

STRAWBERRY KEY LIME PIE MARTINI

1 ½ oz (6 counts) Vanilla Vodka
¾ oz (3 counts) Strawberry puree
½ oz (2 counts) Pineapple puree
¼ oz (1 count) Whipped Cream
1 Squeeze of Lime

1 Watermelon

PREPARATION:
Fill shaker with ice. While the shaker is chilling start pouring into the mixing glass all the ingredients as listed. Shake energetically, stir and pour the drink in a chilled martini glass, once the drink is ready slowly pour in strawberry syrup. This is going to be placed on the bottom of the glass creating a great visual effect.

The color is opaque rose with a rich smell of the fresh strawberries and the whipped cream. The taste is warm, well balanced, a dry/sweet clean finish.

LA STORIA

Everyone has heard of the Italian concept of Hospitaliano. In Italia, it is part of the cultural standard to love your guests. Not just enjoy them, but to have genuine love for them, both as human beings, and as people you are sharing company and a piece of your life with. Who wouldn't want to make every part of a life that is shared with others as memorable and enjoyable as possible? This is especially true if you are the guest and an Italian is the host. Italians are best when hosting. When someone has decided to spend an evening with us, drinking our spirits and eating our food, what greater honor could there be? We want these people to be happy and feel they are wanted, that they are welcome, that they are loved! This, my friends, is the Italian concept of Hospitaliano!

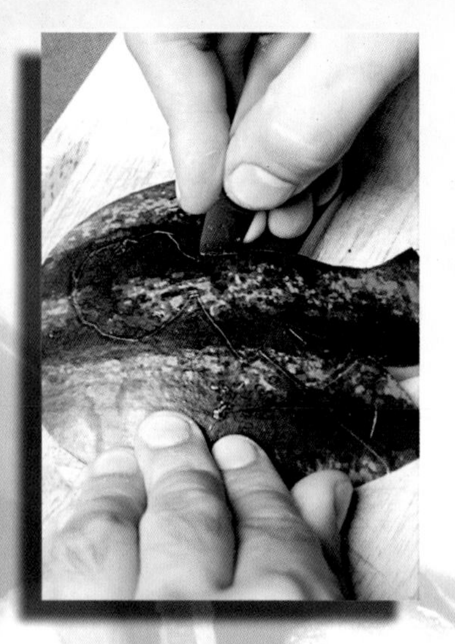

Using a watermelon skin canvas and a paring knife, cut a stencil of your boy figure into the canvas.

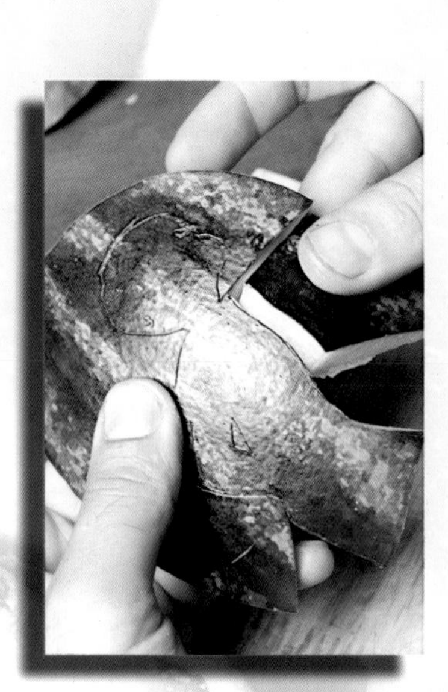

Carefully cut and remove excess canvas from the "neck" downward and removing at the base of our garnish.

Now, cut from the back, around the "arm" of our garnish up to the "head."

Finally, cut around the head, and then make two very small wedges to finish the "hairline."

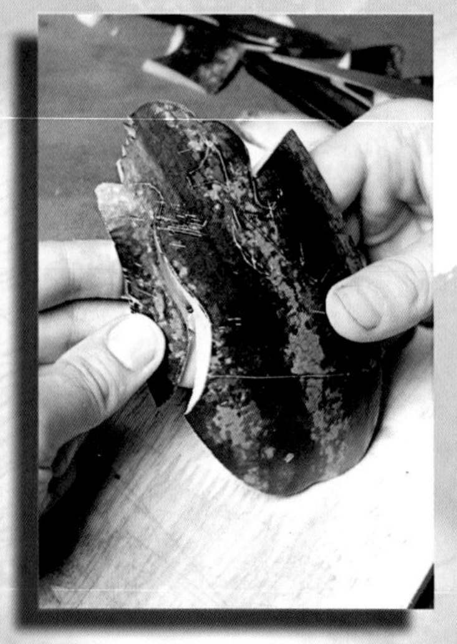

With a second piece of canvas, and your paring knife, outline the girl figure and start with the face.

Cut around the eyebrows, down to the lips, then around the chin, and finally down the front.

Continue to cut from the bottom around the hand, and remove just shy from the ponytail.

Carefully cut around the ponytail and remove to complete your girl garnish.

Work? I never worked a day in my life because I always loved what I was doing and had a passion for it!

__Jacopo Falleni

We have been so blessed in our journey in this country. Fabio and I feel like we have won the lottery for Italians in America! When we talk of our time here and of all the amazing things that have happened, the one that stands out the most is...the people. The one thing we both know is that we could never have accomplished any of this without the people who work with us and for us! Our staff at Café Firenze is more than staff, they are our friends. More than friends, they truly are our famiglia!

When people come to Café Firenze, all of the faces that you see are what makes us who we are. All of the Firenze Family make up the very spirit of the Italian Hospitaliano. We all share in common the desire to make your Firenze experience as if we had whisked you away from your lives here, directly to the rolling slopes of Tuscany. It is our wish that we give you every taste of Italia while you are in our home at Firenze! There are too many people to mention individually, but all of you who are our family, know how you are! Together we are a family! Together nothing can stop us! Together, we are Café Firenze.

Café Firenze
ABEL SORIANO
SOUS CHEF
Café Firenze
JOHN PAOLONE
EXECUTIVE CHEF
FABIO VIVIANI
true

John Paolone

Chef John's passion for Italian cooking began at a very young age. As the son of Italian descendents from Abruzzo, Italy, he was taught traditional cuisine and techniques by his grandparents.

John graduated in 2001 from the Santa Barbara Culinary School and from Le Cordon Bleu Culinary Institute in Pasadena in 2003. He also attended an extensive culinary program in Florence, Italy to expand his knowledge of Italian cooking.

After graduating, John quickly became the Executive Chef at Café Fiore, an Italian Restaurant in downtown Ventura, and then moved to become the Chef at Saticoy Country Club.

He has been working as the Executive Chef at Café Firenze since its opening in 2007. As Executive Chef, John is a fan of making everything from the freshest and highest quality ingredients. In doing so, he chooses to import ingredients and products from Italy for the sake of keeping things traditional. Among other things, Chef John enjoys making braised meats in rich sauces that bring out the true flavor of Italy. "My favorite dish by far is the braised veal Shank, the Osso Buco. Nothing says Italy better than a ten-hour braised veal shank," says John.

Confident in his work ethic, and style of cooking, Chef John Paolone feels nothing on this planet can stop him from providing high-quality meals to the true "foodie" in all of us.

Teaming up with Fabio, these two Troublemakers are planning to take over United States, one meal at time.

THE END

GLOSSARY

Al Dente: Cooked just enough to retain a firm texture.
Amaretto di Saronno: Italian liqueur flavored with herbs and fruits soaked in apricot kernel oil
Balsamic Vinegar: Aged Italian vinegar - from must of white grapes.
Banana liqueur: A sweet, rich banana flavored liqueur
Basil: Amomatic herb of the mint family used dried or fresh for seasoning.
Bernaise: Sauce made of clarified butter, egg yolks, flavored with tarragon and shallots.
Blackberry Vodka: Vodka with the zing of blackberries
Blanch: Boil in water to stop enzymatic action.
Bloom: Mix gelatin with liquid to hydrate.
Caipirinia: Traditionally prepared with lime, brown sugar cubes, crushed ice and a large shot of finest Cachacha Pitu.
Calamari: Squid that has been prepared for seafood dishes.
Campari: An alcoholic aperitif obtained from the infusion of bitter herbs, aromatic plants and fruit in alcohol and water.
Celery salt: A flavored salt used as a food seasoning, made from ground seeds, which come from celery and mix with salt.
Chachaca: The product of the distillation of fermented sugarcane juice, with its alcohol strength anywhere from 38% to 80%
Chai Syrup: Full-bodied blend of exotic teas and spices made into a syrup.
Chamomile: Eurasion herb naturalized in North America.
Chia: Amromatic tea, Mde with herbs or spices, used in foods, teas or lattes.
Cinnamon: Aromatic spice prepared from the dried inner bark of a cinnamon tree.
Cipollini Onions: Small onion, about the size of ping pong balls, with flat tops.
Citrus Vodka: A citrus-flavored vodka made with the addition of lemon and other citrus fruits
Clam: Edible bivalve mollusk that lives in mud or sand.
Coconut Rum: Coconut flavored rum
Cognac balloon glass: Often referred to as a Brandy snifter, with a bulbous balloon-style bowl for drinkers to inhale the aromas of brandy or other cognac wines.
Cointreau: A unique spirit combined with the subtle harmony of bitter and sweet oranges
Confit: Goose, duck or pork that has been cooked in its own fat.
Cornish Hen: English breed of domestic fowl used for food purposes.
Counts: Method of measuring used to dispense precise amount of liquid from bottle using a poor spout. Each count is equal to ¼ oz
Cream Cheese: Mild soft unripened cheese made from whole sweet milk enriched with cream.
Demi Glace': Made from brown stock thatn has been reduced to an intense, flavorful glaze.
Dry Vermouth: A fortified white wine, infused, distilled or macerated with herbs, spices, caramel and other ingredients.
Elderflowers: A genus of of shrubs in the moschatel family, Adoxaceae which bears large clusters of small black, blue-black, or red berries.
Escolar: Large rough scaled fish that resembles mackrel.
Espresso: A concentrated coffee beverage brewed by forcing hot water under pressure through finely ground coffee
Extra Virgin Olive Oil: Oil from first pressing of the olives.
Fleur de Sel: Hand raked and harvester in France,usually from top layer of the salt bed only,
Garlic: European bulbous herb of the lily family cultivated for its pungent compound bulbs used in cooking.
Gelatin: Edible jelly like substance made from various proteins.
Ginger: Pungent aromatic rhizome used as a spice. The underground stem of the ginger plant, Zingiber officinale
Gnocchi: Dumpling made of potato or semolina served with a sauce.
Goblet glass: A clear, thin, stemmed glass with an elongated oval bowl tapering inward at the rim
Godiva Caramel Liqueur: A blend of milk chocolate and caramel flavored liqueur.
Gorgonzola Cheese: Pungent blue cheese of Italian origin.
Gelatin: Edible jelly like substance made from various proteins.
Ginger: Pungent aromatic rhizome used as a spice. The underground stem of the ginger plant, Zingiber officinale
Gnocchi: Dumpling made of potato or semolina served with a sauce.
Goblet glass: A clear, thin, stemmed glass with an elongated oval bowl tapering inward at the rim
Godiva Caramel Liqueur: A blend of milk chocolate and caramel flavored liqueur.
Gorgonzola Cheese: Pungent blue cheese of Italian origin.

GLOSSARY

Half and Half: Mixture of half cream and half whole milk.
Heavy Cream: Cream that by law contains no less than 36% butterfat.
Idaho Potatoes: Baking type potato high in starch - also good for frying.
Italian Style Bloody Mary Mix: Take 3 Celery Sticks, 2 basil leaves, and 1 garlic clove. Cut them in small pieces. Add ¼ oz of Tomato Vodka so the celery can absorb all the flavors. You can add instead of the garlic and the basil, a teaspoon of pesto sauce. The color won't be as inviting but the taste will be phenomenal. Leave it in maceration for a couple of hours. Add 5 dashes of Worcestershire Sauce, one espresso spoon each of mustard and Tabasco (depending on how spicy you like it!) ½ oz of fresh lime juice, and salt and pepper to taste.
Jalapeño: Small plump dark green Mexican hot pepper.
Kahlua: A Mexican coffee-flavored liqueur
Kennebec Potatoes: Boiling potato, high in sugar and low in starch -holds shape in cooking.
Kosher Salt: A salt that is ritually fit for use according to Jewish law.
Lemon Peel: An intensely flavored lemon zest prepared by gently carving strips from the peel from a lemon
Linguine: Narrow, flat pasta.
Lobster: Large edible marine decapod crustacean - has large claws and a long abdomen.
Lychee: (Also litchi.)The oval fruit of a tree from the soapberry family that has a reddish outer covering and sweet white inner flesh.
Mahi-mahi: Dolphin used for food.
Marsala wine: A sweet wine produced in the region surrounding the Italian city of Marsala in Sicily.
Mascarpone Cheese: Italian cream cheese.
Microplane: Also called grater or zester: a small hand held tool that comes in coarse, fine and spice blades.
Miso Paste: A fermented paste of cooked soybeans, salt,and barley or rice.
Muddle: Mix, mash or stir thoroughly, creating a thick substance.
Mussels: Marine bivalve mollusk with dark elongated shell - used in seafood dishes.
Nutmeg: An aromatic seed used as a spice - usually grated or ground.
Old fashion glass: Short tumbler used for serving an alcoholic beverage, such as whiskey
Paring knife: A small knife with a plain edge blade that is ideal for peeling and other small or intricate work
Pancetta: Unsmoked belly meat used in Italian dishes.
Paprika: Mild red condiment consisting of the dried finely ground pods of various sweet peppers.
Parchment Paper: Heavy paper used for wrapping foods for cooking, lining pans for baking, etc.
Parmesan Cheese: A very hard, dry sharply flavored cheese sold grated or in wedges.
Peach liqueur: A peach-flavored aperitif
Pear Nectar: Unstrained juice from pears
Pepper Vodka: Vodka insinuated with the aroma of herbs and the taste of red chili pepper
Peppercorn: Dried berry of the black pepper.
Pesto: A sauce whose name is the contracted past participle of pestâ, to pound or crush, in reference to the sauce's crushed herbs and garlic.
Pine Nut: Edible sed of several varieties of pines.
Poach: Cook in a simmering liquid.
Polenta: Made from a finely ground meal - corn, farina, semolina, etc.
Pomegranate: Thick skinned red fruit with many seeds inside. Juice is tart.
Port wine: A sweet red wine, also comes in dry, semi-dry and white varieties. It is often served as a dessert wine
Poussin: Chicken bred specifically to produce small consistent sized birds ready for harvest quickly.
Prawn: Edible crustacean that resembles a large shrimp.
Prosciutto: Dry cured, spiced Italian ham.
Ramekin: Small individual baking dish.
Ravioli: Pasta formed to pockets that contain a savory filling of meat or cheese.
Reduction: The amount by which something (usually a liquid) is lessened - 1/2, 1/3, etc.
Ricotta Cheese: A white unripened whey cheese of Italy that resembles cottage cheese.
Rosemary: Fragrant shrubby mint of southern Europe and Asia Minor. The leaves are used as seasoning.
Roux: Cooked mixture of flour and fat used in soups and sauces.

GLOSSARY

Russett Potatoes : Baking type potato high in starch - also good for frying.
Sage: An herb with a slight peppery flavor, with woody stems, grayish leaves, and blue to purplish flower
Seabass: Food and sport fish - smaller and ore active than grouper.
Sear: Brown quickly over intense heat.
Shallot: Bulbous perennial herb that resembles an onion. Produces small clusters of bulbs used for cooking.
Shrimp: Edible marine decapods crustacean with elongated body - excellent in seafood preparations.
Snapper: Carnivorous fish - important in seafood dishes.
Spaghetti squash: An oblong seed-bearing variety of winter squash
Squab: A fledging pigeon, about four weeks old.
St Germain Liqueur: liqueur made from wild elderflowers
Stem less martini glass: Martini glass without a stem
Swordfish: Large bony fish with a sword like beak - important food and game fish.
Tabasco: A brand of hot sauce made from tabasco peppers, vinegar, and salt, and aged in white oak barrels for three years.
Taro root: Tropical plant grown as a vegetable food and secondarily as a leaf vegetable - believed to be one of the earliest cultivated plants.
Tenderloin: Pork or beef strip, very tender, that comes for the area next to the vertebral column.
Tequila: An agave-based spirit made primarily in the area surrounding the city of Tequila.
Thyme: Eurasian mint family with small aromatic leaves used as a culinary herb and a groundcover, and has a very strong caraway scent due to the chemical carvone
Tilapia: Chiclid found in warm waters, usually Africa and farmed in US - Good food product.
Tomato Vodka: Vodka infused with the tastes of tomatoes, pepper, horseradish and spices
Triplesec: An orange-flavored liqueur made from the dried peel of oranges from the Caribbean. Its name means triple distilled.
Truffle: The buried fruit of several European fungi.
Tuna: Large vigorous scombroid food and sport fish - Albacore, Bluefin, Yellow, etc.
Vanilla Bean: Long capsular fruit from the epiphytic orchid, used for flavoring foods.
Vanilla rum: Rum enriched with natural vanilla flavor
Vanilla Vodka: Vodka infused with Vanilla flavoring
Vermouth Rosso: A fortified wine flavoured with aromatic herbs and using closely guarded recipes
Vinaigrette: Sauce or dressing made fro oil, vinegar, onions,parsley and herbs - typically used on cold meats. Fish or salads
Wasabi: Member of the Brassicaceae family. Known as "Japanese horseradish", its root is used as a spice and has an extremely strong flavour.
Wasabi Paste: Condiment prepared from the thick pungent greenish root of an asian herb of the mustart family. Similar in flavor and use to horseradish.
Worchester: A fermented liquid condiment first made by two dispensing chemists, John Wheeley Lea and William Henry Perrins in 1837.
Zen liquor: Produced using only the finest ingredients, with a perfectly balanced blend of specially selected Kyoto green tea leaves
Zest: A thin layer of the outer skin of lemon or orange used as flavoring.
Zucchini Squash: Formerly often referred to as green Italian squash, a variety of summer squash developed in Italy

INDEX

INDEX

INDEX